KB139968

College 2
English

College English 2

정효숙 지음

　이 책은 영어 기초가 부족한 학생과 성인들이 영어를 쉽게 공부할 수 있도록 구성하였다. 그리하여 문법이나 어휘가 부족한 학생들도 영어에 흥미와 자신감을 갖게 하는 것이 이 책의 목표이다. 각 단원들은 최근의 사회적 이슈나 문제들에 관해 독해 부분과 회화 부분으로 구성하였다.

　독해 부분과 회화 부분에 대해 각각 해석과 주요 어휘를 정리하였다. 또한 영어의 주요 문법이나 문장 구조를 잘 이해할 수 있도록 상세한 설명과 예문을 제시하였다. 그리하여 혼자서도 이 책을 공부할 수 있게 하였다.

　각 단원의 이야기는 쉬운 문장을 사용하고 있어서 영어에 자신이 없는 사람도 어려움이나 지루함을 느끼지 않게 하였다. 이 책을 공부하는 방법은 해석과 구문을 모두 이해한 후에 거꾸로 한글로 된 해석을 보고 영어로 다시 쓰거나 말할 수 있도록 공부하는 것이 좋다. 독해로 이루어진 문장이 어려우면 회화체 내용을 중심으로 학습

하는 것도 좋은 방법이다. 그리하면 현 사회의 이슈들에 대해서 내국인이나 외국인 혹은 어떤 단체의 면접관 앞에서도 영어로 의견을 자유자재로 피력할 수 있는 능력과 자신감을 기를 수 있을 것이다. 부디 이 책을 통하여 사회적 문제를 쉬운 영어로도 표현할 수 있는 방식을 익혀서 글로벌 시대에 영어로 자신의 생각을 적극적으로 표현할 수 있는 사람이 되기를 바란다.

CONTENTS

01 My biggest problem in school

학교에서 나의 가장 큰 문제

Reading Comprehension

My biggest problem in school is my lack of self-confidence. I tend to feel that ① everyone else in class knows more than I do, has a better background, and is sharper, more articulate, and wiser. ② I hate to be called on by the teacher. To prevent having to speak up in class, ③ I try to make myself invisible, hid behind hands, lower my eyes, sink down in my chair, and sit in the back of the room. ④ Very often I know the answers to the questions being asked, but I never raise my hand, never volunteer, and never open my mouth willingly.

학교에서 나의 가장 큰 문제점은 자신감이 없다는 것이다. 나는 우리 반에서 다른 사람들이 나보다 더 많이 알고, 더 나은 배경을 갖고 있고, 더 날카롭고, 더 명료하고, 더 현명하다고 생각하는 경향이 있다. 나는 선생님에게 지명당하는 것을 싫어한다. 학급에서 발표하는 것을 피하기 위해서 나는 내 자신을 드러내지 않고 다른 사람들 뒤에 숨고, 눈을 아래로 깔고, 의자에 낮게 앉고, 교실 뒤쪽에 앉으려고 노력한다. 자주 질문에 대한 대답을 아주 잘 알고 있지만 손을 든 적도 없고, 자발적이었던 적도 없으며, 내 입을 의도적으로 열려고 하지도 않는다.

■ Words & Phrases

lack: 부족, 결핍, ~이 없다
tend to: ~하는 경향이 있다
self-confidence: 자신감
articulate: (말, 발음 등이) 명료한, 또렷하게 발음된, 분명한
call on: ~에게 청하다, 요구하다, 부탁하다, …을 방문하다
prevent: 막다, 예방하다
speak up: 큰소리로 이야기하다
invisible: 모습을 나타내지 않는, 눈에 안 보이는
volunteer: 자진하여 하다, 자발적으로 말하다
willingly: 자진해서, 기꺼이

■ Grammatical Points

① everyone else in class knows more than I do, has a better background, and is sharper, more articulate, and wiser.

: 주어는 everyone else in class(학급에 있는 그 외의 모든 사람들)이고 everyone은 3인칭 단수 취급을 함으로 동사는 knows, has, is이다.

② I hate to be called on by the teacher.

: 'be called on'은 수동태로 '불리어지다'의 뜻이다.

③ I try to make myself invisible, hid behind hands, lower my eyes, sink down in my chair, and sit in the back of the room.

: make는 사역동사이고 myself는 목적어, invisible, hid는 목적보어이다. 동사는 try, lower, sink, sit이다.

④ Very often I know the answers to the questions being asked,

: 'the answers to'는 '～에 대한 답'이란 뜻이고, 'the questions (which are) being asked'에서는 which are가 생략되었고 '질문되어지고 있는 문제들'이란 뜻이다.

Speaking Practice

A: Do you know what the most important _____ of a successful person is?

성공하는 사람의 가장 중요한 자질이 뭔지 아니?

B: I'm not ____, but I think _____ is the key to success.

확실히는 모르겠지만 나는 정직이 성공의 열쇠라고 생각해.

A: You know what everybody says nowadays?

요즘 사람들이 뭐라고 이야기하는지 아니?

B: I don't know. What?

몰라, 뭔데?

A: Creativity is the ____ to success.

창의성이 성공의 열쇠다.

B: I guess you're right. I'm afraid I'm not a very _____ person.

네 말이 맞아. 난 창의적인 사람이 아닌 것 같아 걱정이야.

A: You just have to find your _____ talents.

너는 너의 숨겨진 재능을 찾아야 해.

B: What do you think my hidden _____ are?

나의 숨겨진 재능이 뭐라고 생각하니?

A: I think you're ＿＿＿ at writing and making stories.

너는 글을 쓰고 이야기 만드는 걸 잘하는 것 같아.

■ Words & Phrases

quality: 질, 품질, 자질, 속성
nowadays: 오늘날, 요즈음에는
key: 열쇠, 비결, 해법
honesty: 정직
creativity: 창조력, 독창물
hidden talent: 숨겨진 재능
be good at: ~을 잘하다

■ Grammatical Points

Do you know what the most important quality of a successful person is?

: what the most important quality of a successful person is는 know의 목적어로 쓰인 간접의문문이다. 간접의문문은 '의문사+주어+동사'의 어순이다.

You know what everybody says nowadays?

: what everybody says nowadays는 know의 목적어로 쓰인 간접의

문문이다. 간접의문문은 '의문사+주어+동사'의 어순이다.

What do you think my hidden talents are?

: 간접의문문에서 think, believe, imagine, guess, suppose 등의 동사가 쓰일 때는 의문사가 문장의 맨 앞에 놓인다.

e.g. Who do you think he is? (너는 그가 누구라고 생각하니?)

I think honesty is the key to success.

: I think (that) honesty is the key to success. 접속사 that이 생략되었다. 'key to~'는 '~에 대한 비결, 해법'이다.

Unit
02

Koreans hold a mix of hope, concern about a centenarian society

한국인 100세 시대, 희망과 걱정 뒤섞여

Reading Comprehension

① Many Koreans who hope to purse a longer life are still underprepared for the realities of growing old. Thanks to advancements in medical technology, bio science and the social security system, ② the average life expectancy of Koreans is expected to rise to 90 by

2100, from 81.3 in 2012. ③ Asia's fourth-largest economy will also become a "super-aged society" by 2026 when the proportion of people aged 65 and over is expected to surpass the 20 percent mark. The demographic forecast is expected to bring tremendous changes to every facet of society from politics and the economy to culture and leisure.

오래 살기를 바라는 많은 한국인들이 노령화의 현실적 문제에 대해서는 여전히 준비가 부족하다. 의료기술과 생명과학, 사회 안전보장제도의 발전 덕분에 한국인의 평균 기대수명이 2012년 81.3세에서 2100년 90세로 늘어날 전망이다. 경제 규모가 아시아 4위인 한국은 65세 이상 노인 비중이 전체 인구의 20%를 초과할 2026년이 되면 초고령 사회로 진입할 전망이다. 이러한 인구통계의 예측은 정치 경제부터 문화 레저까지 사회 전 분야에 대변화를 초래할 것으로 예상된다.

■ Words & Phrases

hold: 지니다
mix: 혼합
concern: 걱정
centenarian: 100세의
purse: 추구하다
underprepared: 준비가 불충분한
reality: 현실
advancement: 발전
technology: 과학기술

bio science: 생명과학
thanks to: ~덕분에
is expected to: ~으로 기대되다
social security system: 사회 안전보장제도
average life expectancy: 평균 기대수명
super-aged: 초고령
surpass: 능가하다
demographic: 인구통계학의
tremendous: 엄청난
facet: 측면, 양상
politics: 정치
from A to B: A에서부터 B까지

■ Grammatical Points

① Many Koreans who hope to purse a longer life are still underprepared for the realities of growing old.

: who는 주격 관계대명사로 who hope to purse a longer life가 앞에 있는 many Koreans를 수식한다. 따라서 장수를 추구하는 많은 한국인이 주어이다. 주어가 복수이므로 동사는 are이다. be underprepared for는 '~가 준비되지 않다'의 뜻이다.

② the average life expectancy of Koreans is expected to rise to 90 by 2100,

: is expected는 수동태(be 동사+p.p.)로 '기대되다'라는 의미이다. by는 '까지'의 뜻이다.

③ Asia's fourth-largest economy will also become a "super-aged society" by 2026 when the proportion of people aged 65 and over is expected to surpass the 20 percent mark.

: when은 때를 나타내는 관계부사로 when the proportion of people aged 65 and over is expected to surpass the 20 percent mark이 2026을 수식한다.

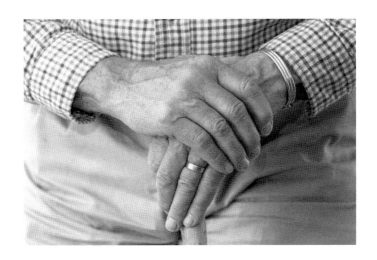

Speaking Practice

A: Do you know what an _____ society is?

넌 고령사회가 뭔지 아니?

B: If the _____ of seniors aged 65 or older _____ the total population is over 14%, it is considered an aged society.

전체 인구에서 65세 혹은 그 이상의 노인 비율이 14% 이상이면, 고령사회로 간주되지.

A: What _____ Korea? Are we an aged society or an _____ society?

한국은 어떠니? 우리는 고령사회야 아니면 고령화 사회야?

B: Korea became an aging society in 2000. But we are _____ the status of "aged society" very rapidly.

한국은 2000년에 고령화 사회에 진입했어. 그렇지만 매우 급속도로 고령사회로 접근하고 있어.

A: Wow. You seem very _____ about that.

와, 너 그것에 대해 정말 많이 알고 있는 것 같다.

B: In fact, I just read about in the newspaper. Experts _____ Korea will become an aged society in 19 years.

사실, 신문에서 그것에 대해 읽었어. 그리고 전문가들이 한국은 19년 후면 고령사회가 된다고 예측해.

A: Are other countries aging as _____ as ours?

다른 나라들도 우리처럼 그렇게 빨리 늙고 있는 거니?

B: No, it says that it _____ 24 years for Japan ___ change from an aging to an aged society and 115 years for France. So I guess we are a rapidly aging group.

아니, 일본은 고령화 사회에서 고령사회로 바뀌는 데 24년, 프랑스는 115년이 걸렸대. 그러니까 우리가 상당히 빠른 그룹에 속하는 거지.

■ Words & Phrases

aged: 노령의, 나이 먹은
senior: 손위의, 선배의, 상관
ratio: 비, 비율
against: ~에 대조하여, ~에 대비하여
total: 전체의, 통계의
consider: ~이라고 생각하다, 간주하다
aging society: 고령화 사회
approach: 접근하다
status: 사정, 사태, 지위
knowledgeable: 잘 아는, 총명한
rapidly: 빠르게

■ Grammatical Points

Do you know what an aged society is?

: 간접의문문 문장이다. Do you know+What is an aged society? 가 연결된 문장이다.

It is considered an aged society.

: 수동태 문장으로서 '고령사회로 여겨지다'의 뜻이다.

Are other countries aging as quickly as ours?

: age가 동사로서 '늙어가다, 나이를 먹다'의 뜻이다. as quickly as는 동등비교이고 ours는 our country의 뜻이다.

Unit

03 What are the advantages of a Cellphone?

휴대폰의 이점은 무엇인가?

Reading Comprehension

Nowadays the cellphone has gotten very popular, and almost everyone has one. ① It has become so inseparable that it sometimes feels like your best friend. Most of all, ② it is one of the most convenient tools for entertainment. Besides making phone calls, you can send messages, take pictures, listen to music or access the Internet anytime you want. You will be never bored when you have a cellphone with you.

In addition, ③ it offers you more safety. When you are in trouble, you can call someone to help you right away. In fact, a cellphone once saved a kidnapped boy. When his kidnapper was not watching, the boy called the police using his cellphone and was rescued. Therefore, ④ we should make the best use of this creature of modern technology.

오늘날 휴대폰은 매우 대중적이 되었다. 그리하여 거의 모든 사람이 한 개는 가지고 있다. 그것은 떨어질 수 없게 되어서 가끔은 제일 친한 친구처럼 느껴진다.

무엇보다도 그것은 오락을 위한 가장 편리한 기구 중의 하나이다. 전화를 거는 것 외에 메시지를 보내고 사진을 찍고 음악을 듣고 혹은 원하는 아무 때나 인터넷에 접속할 수 있다. 휴대폰을 가지고 있을 때는 절대 지루하지 않다.

게다가 그것은 당신에게 더 많은 안전을 제공한다. 당신이 어려움에 처해 있을 때 도와달라고 누군가에게 즉시 전화를 할 수 있다. 실제로, 휴대폰이 언젠가 유괴된 소년을 구했었다. 유괴범이 보고 있지 않을 때 소년은 그의 휴대폰을 이용하여 경찰에 전화를 하여 구출되었다. 그러므로 우리는 현대 과학기술의 이 산물을 잘 이용해야 한다.

■ Words & Phrases

inseparable: 나눌 수 없는, 분리할 수 없는
most of all: 무엇보다도
tool: 도구
besides: 게다가, 그 외에
access: 접근하다, 접속하다
bored: 지루한
in addition: 게다가
offer: 제공하다
right away: 즉시
once: 이전에, 언젠가, 한번은
kidnapper: 유괴자, 납치자
rescue: 구출하다
make use of: ~을 이용하다
creature: (신의 창조물) 산물
technology: 과학기술

■ Grammatical Points

① **It has become so inseparable that it sometimes feels like your best friend.**

: 'so… that~'는 '너무 …해서~하다'의 뜻이다. feel like는 '~처럼 느끼다'의 뜻이다.

② **it is one of the most convenient tools for entertainment.**

: 'one of+the 복수명사'는 '~들 중 하나이다'의 뜻이다.

③ **it offers you more safety.**

: offer는 수여동사(4형식 동사)로 'offer+간접목적어(사람)+직

접목적어(사물)'의 구문이다. 3형식 문장인 'it offers more safety to you'로 바꾸어 쓸 수 있다.

④ **we should make the best use of this creature of modern technology.**

: make use of는 '~을 이용하다'의 뜻이고 make the best use of는 '가장 잘 이용해야 하다'라는 뜻이다.

Speaking Practice

A: Excuse me, My phone stopped _____ yesterday all of a sudden
and I am not sure _____. Do you think you could take a ____
at it?

실례합니다. 제 전화기가 어제 갑자기 멈췄는데, 이유가 확실치
않습니다. 잠시 살펴봐 주실 수 있나요?

B: Have you tried _____ it?

재설정 해보셨나요?

A: Resetting it? Oh no, I haven't actually. How do you reset
Nokia phones anyway?

재설정이요? 아, 아니요. 사실 안 해 봤어요. 노키아 전화를 어
떻게 재설정하죠?

B: You just have to _____ these two side buttons at the _____

time and there you have it. It should come on now. Aha, there

you go. Everything should be working again now.

측면의 2개의 버튼을 동시에 눌러 주시기만 하면 돼요. 지금 해

보죠. 아하, 잘 됐습니다. 이제 모든 게 다시 잘 작동될 겁니다.

A: That's ___? Wow, you really have the magic touch. Thank you

so much.

다 된 건가요? 와우, 대단하세요. 정말 감사합니다.

■ **Words & Phrases**

work: 작동하다
all of a sudden: 갑자기
take a look at: ~을 보다
reset: 다시 (고쳐)놓다
press: 누르다
at the same time: 동시에
there you go: 자, 바라, 말한 대로지
magic: 마술의

■ **Grammatical Points**

My phone stopped working.

: stop 다음에는 목적어로 동명사가 온다.

Have you tried resetting it?

: 'try+동명사'는 '~을 해보다'라는 뜻이다.

That's it?

: '이것으로 끝이야?'라는 뜻이다.

You just have to press these two side buttons.

: 이 두 사이드 버튼을 누르기만 해야 한다.

※ **형용사의 어순**

· 형용사의 위치는 보통 '**관사+부사+형용사+명사**'의 순으로 되지만, 두 개 이상의 형용사가 쓰이면 그 순서는 '**관사(또는 지시형용사)+수량형용사+성 상형용사+명사**'로 된다.

   e.g. This si an interesting book.
      This is a very interesting book.
      Those two tall boys are her sons.
      (저 두 명의 키 큰 소년은 그녀의 아들이다.)

everything should be working again now

: should는 '[확실성, 가능성 있는 미래](틀림없이)~일게다'의 뜻이다.

  e.g. They should arrive by one o'clock, I think.

     (한 시 안으로 도착할 겁니다.)

Unit

04 Koreans' insurance

한국인들의 보험 문화

Reading Comprehension

Most people in Korea buy their insurance through relatives, friends, and acquaintances. Even though they don't see any immediate need for it, ① they buy it in order to maintain their personal or official relationship with the salesman. In this way, many people feel a lot of social pressure to buy insurance. ② I know this is dangerous as well as wrong. ③ We must buy insurance based on our needs and benefits, not because of personal relationships.

대부분의 한국에 사는 사람들은 친척이나 지인들을 통해 보험에 가입한다. 비록 그들은 보험에 대해 어떤 직접적인 필요를 인식하지 못해도 판매자와 그들의 개인적인 관계를 유지하기 위해 그것들을 산다. 이런 방법으로, 많은 사람들이 보험을 사도록 강요받는다. 난 이것이 위험할 뿐만 아니라 잘못되었다는 것을 안다. 우리는 보험을 개인적인 관계가 아닌 우리의 필요와 이익에 기반해서 사야 한다.

■ Words & Phrases

insurance: 보험
through: ~을 통하여
relatives: 친척
acquaintances: 아는 사람, 지인
even though: 비록~일지라도
immediate: 직접적인, 즉시의
in order to: ~하기 위하여
maintain: 유지하다
A as well as B: B뿐만 아니라 A
relationship: 관계
in this way: 이런 식으로
pressure: 압력
based on: ~에 기초를 두다
benefit: 이익

■ Grammatical Points

① they buy it in order to maintain their personal or official relationship with the salesman.

: in order to maintain 대신에 to maintain을 써도 된다.

② I know this is dangerous as well as wrong.

: I know 뒤에 접속사 that이 생략되었다. dangerous as well as wrong은 not only wrong but also dangerous와 같은 뜻이다. 잘못되었을 뿐만 아니라 위험하다.

③ We must buy insurance based on our needs and benefits,

: insurance (which is) based on our needs and benefits의 문장이다. 주격 관계대명사 (which+be 동사)가 생략되었다.

Speaking Practice

A: What do you usually ___ on weekends?

당신은 주말에 대체로 무엇을 합니까?

B: Nothing _____. I stay home all ____.

특별한 것은 없습니다. 하루 종일 집에 있습니다.

A: Don't you go ____?

외출은 하지 않습니까?

B: Rarely. I'm usually ___ tired ___ go out. Besides, Sunday is my only day ___, so I have to clean the house, do the _____ and other _____.

좀처럼요. 대체로 너무 피곤해서 외출할 수가 없습니다. 게다가,

일요일은 유일하게 쉬는 날이니까, 집 청소를 한다거나, 세탁이나 그 외의 잡무를 보지 않으면 안 됩니다.

A: The Koreans work too hard. I feel _____ for you.

한국인은 지나치게 일을 많이 합니다. 딱해요.

B: But I _____ to stay home and do little things around the house. I especially enjoy _____ in my garden. I _____ many kinds of flowers.

하지만 나는 집에서, 집안의 여기저기 잡다한 일을 하는 것을 좋아합니다. 특히 나는 정원에서 일하는 것을 좋아합니다. 많은 종류의 꽃을 기르고 있습니다.

■ Words & Phrases

weekend: 주말
weekday: 주중
all day: 하루 종일
rarely: 좀처럼~하지 않다
besides: 게다가
day off: 휴일
chore: 잡일, 잡다한 일
feel sorry for: ~을 가엾게 여기다
prefer (like better): 더 좋아하다
around: 여기저기
expecially: 특히
grow: 키우다

■ Grammatical Points

on weekends

: every weekend의 뜻이다.

I'm usually too tired to go out.

: 'too… to~'는 '너무 …해서~할 수 없다.'

Nothing special

: something, anything, everything, nothing을 수식하는 형용사는 그 위에 놓는다.

I especially enjoy working in my garden.

: enjoy 다음에는 동명사가 목적어로 온다.

※ **동명사만을 목적어로 취하는 동사**

mind, enjoy, give up, avoid, finish, escape, deny 등
 e.g. She avoids speaking in public.
　　　(그녀는 사람들 앞에서 말하는 것을 피한다.)
　　　Have you finished sending an e-mail?
　　　(너는 이메일을 쓰는 것을 끝마쳤는가?)
　　　When did you give up studying?
　　　(너는 공부를 언제 포기했니?)
　　　Would you mind opening the window?
　　　(창문 좀 열어 주시겠어요?)

‖ 주의 ‖　이때의 mind는 '싫어하다, 꺼리다'란 뜻이므로, 답할 때에는 Of
　　　　course not, 혹은 I'm sorry I can't로 한다.

05 Who invented Ramen first?

누가 라면을 처음 발명했을까?

Reading Comprehension

① What is the most popular food in the world? Rice is at the top of the list, followed by bread. Unbelievably, ramen comes in third. How often do you eat ramen? According to statistics, ② Korea ranks fifth in ramen consumption followed by China, Indonesia, Japan, and America.

Ramen was invented by a Japanese man named Momofuku Ando. Traditionally, the Japanese enjoyed ramen, but it was not instant ramen. Ando wanted to change traditional ramen into instant ramen. He wanted to provide food that was cheap and easy to make.

One day, ③ Ando discovered how he could make instant noodles that could be preserved for a long time. Like fried food, he fried raw noodles at a high temperature for a short time. ④ This caused the moisture in the noodles to evaporate instantly, leaving holes in the noodles. And the noodles regain their original shape when they are boiled.

Finally, he developed the first instant noodles in 1958. People could enjoy the ramen after boiling it for two minutes. Then in 1971, he released the world's first "cup noodles."

세계에서 가장 인기 있는 음식은 무엇일까? 쌀이 일등, 빵이 그 뒤를 이었다. 놀랍게도, 라면이 3등이다. 당신은 얼마나 자주 라면을 먹는가? 통계에 따르면, 한국은 라면 소비에 있어서 중국, 인도네시아, 일본, 미국에 이어 5번째이다.

라면은 안도 모모후쿠라는 일본인이 발명했다. 전통적으로, 일본인들은 라면을 즐겨 먹었지만, 인스턴트 라면이 아니었다. 안도는 전통적인 라면을 인스턴트 라면으로 바꾸고 싶었다. 그는 값싸고 만들기 쉬운 음식을 제공하고 싶었다.

어느 날 그는 오랫동안 보존될 수 있는 인스턴트 국수를 만들 수 있는 방법을 발견했다. 튀김 음식처럼, 그는 높은 온도에서 짧은 시간 동안 생면을 튀겼다. 이것은 국수의 수분이 즉시 증발되어 국수에 구멍을 남겼다. 튀긴 국수는 오랜 시간 지속되었다. 그리고 그 국수는 끓으면 원래 모양으로 되돌아왔다.

마침내 그는 1958년에 최초로 인스턴트 국수를 개발했다. 사람들은 2분간 라면을 끓이면 먹을 수 있게 되었다. 그리고 1971년, 그는 세계 최초의 컵라면을 출시했다.

■ Words & Phrases

according to statistics: 통계에 따르면
consumption: 소비
create: 만들다, 창조하다
invent: 발명하다
traditionally: 전통적으로
provide: 제공하다
preserve: 보존하다
cause: 원인이 되다, 야기시키다
moisture: 수분
evaporate: 증발시키다
leave: ～인 채로 두다
regain: 다시 얻다
release: 방출하다

■ Grammatical Points

① What is the most popular food in the world?

: popular의 최상급은 the most popular이다.

② Korea ranks fifth in ramen consumption followed by China,

: consumption 뒤에 (which is)가 생략되었다.

③ Ando discovered how he could make instant noodles that could be preserved for a long time.

: discovered의 목적어로 간접의문문 how+he(주어)+could make (동사) 순으로 되어 있다. that could be preserved for a long time은 instant noodles를 수식한다.

④ This caused the moisture in the noodles to evaporate instantly, leaving holes in the noodles.

: 'cause A to B'는 'A가 B 하도록 야기시키다'의 구문이다. A 는 the moisture in the noodles이고 B는 evaporate instantly이다. leaving은 분사구문으로 and it leaved로 바꿔 쓸 수 있다.

Speaking Practice

A: What's for _____ today?

오늘 점심으로 뭐 먹지?

B: Well··· I have no ____. What would you _____?

글쎄, 모르겠다. 뭘 먹고 싶어?

A: Well. I really feel like seafood spaghetti.

음, 나는 해산물 스파게티가 먹고 싶다.

B: But we are missing one important _____. There's no seafood ____ in the fridge.

근데 우리는 중요한 재료가 하나가 없다. 냉장고에 해산물이 남아 있지 않아.

A: Don't worry. I'll go buy some seafood right now if you decide to make it.

걱정하지 마. 네가 만들려고 결정하면 바로 지금 해산물을 좀 사올게.

B: Okay! I'll do it, but it will _____ at least 30 minutes to _____.

좋아. 할게. 그러나 요리하는 데 적어도 30분이 걸릴 거야.

A: No problem. I'll go to a _____ store right away. Where are the car keys?

괜찮아. 내가 즉시 해산물 가게에 갈게. 자동차 열쇠 어디 있어?

B: On the television in the living room. Ah, go to the store next to the post office. They _____ really fresh seafood.

거실 TV 위에. 아, 우체국 옆에 있는 가게로 가라. 무지 신선한 해산물을 팔거든.

A: Okay, I will.

그럴게.

■ Words & Phrases

feel like: ~하고 싶은 생각이 나다
seafood: 해산물
miss: ~이 없음을 알아채다, 보이지 않다
ingredient: 성분, 재료
fridge: 냉장고
take: (시간이)~걸리다
right away: 즉시, 지금

■ Grammatical Points

There's no seafood left in the fridge.

: There's no seafood (which is) left in the fridge의 뜻으로 left in the fridge가 seafood를 수식한다. leave는 '남다'의 뜻으로 '남은 해산물이 없다'라는 뜻이다.

if you decide to make it.

: decide 다음에는 목적어로 to 부정사가 온다.

※ to 부정사만을 목적어로 취하는 동사

want, hope, decide, plan, promise, choose 등
e.g. I want to be a doctor.
    (나는 의사가 되고 싶다.)
    I have decided to go to America.
    (나는 미국 가기로 결정했다.)
    He promised never to tell a lie.
    (그는 다시는 거짓말을 하지 않기로 약속했다.)

Unit
06 The marriage market

결혼 시장의 변화

Reading Comprehension

The 20 percent of Americans 25 or older are never marrying at all, ① either because they prefer not to, or because they can't find the right person. Young people are more cautious these days, ② whereas lovebirds of yore "used to leap into the uncharted" together. ③ By 2030 nearly 30 percent of American men who were aged between 25-34 in 2010—and 23 percent of women-will not have tied the knot. For men with not much education, the picture is especially grim. Among young American adults with a high school certificate or less, there are 174 never-married men for every 100 never-married women.

　25세 이상의 미국인 20%는 결혼을 원치 않거나 혹은 맞는 사람을 찾지 못해서, 결혼 자체를 하지 않고 있다. 요즈음 젊은이들은 보다 신중해지고 있는 반면, 과거의 잉꼬부부들은 "두 손을 꼭 잡고 미지의 세계에 뛰어들곤 했다"는 것이다. 2030년이 되면, 2010년 당시 25~34세 연령대의 미국 남성들 중 약 30%가 미혼 상태를 유지하고 있을 것이며, 여성들의 경우 이 비율은 23%가 될 것이다. 많은 교육을 받지 않은 남자의 경우, 상황은 더욱 우울하다. 고졸 이하의 학력을 지닌 미국 젊은이들 중 미혼 남녀의 비율은 174 대 100에 달한다.

■ Words & Phrases

either A or B: A나 B 둘 중의 하나
right person: 적당한 사람
cautious: 주의 깊은, 신중한
these days: 요즈음
whereas: 반면에
lovebird: 잉꼬부부
of yore: 과거, 옛날의
leap into A: A에 뛰어들다
uncharted: 지도에 없는
either A or B: A 혹은 B
prefer not to marry: 결혼하지 않는 것을 좋아하다
tied the knot: 결혼하다
grim: 냉혹한, 험악한
certificate: (학력/졸업) 증명서

■ Grammatical Points

① **either because they prefer not to, or because they can't find the right person.**

: 'either because A or because B'는 'A 때문이든가 혹은 B 때문이든지 둘 중의 하나'

② **whereas lovebirds of yore "used to leap into the uncharted" together.**

: 'used to…'는 (과거의) 상태나 습관을 가리킨다.

과거의 잉꼬부부들은 미지의 세계로 함께 뛰어들곤 했다.

③ **By 2030 nearly 30 percent of American men who were aged between 25-34 in 2010-and 23 percent of women-will not have tied the knot.**

: who were aged between 25-34 in 2010이 American men을 수식한다.

will not have tied는 미래 완료동사이다. 따라서 '2030년까지는 결혼을 하지 못할 것이다'라는 뜻이다.

Speaking Practice

Susie: Jane, I can't thank you _____ for the bridal _____ you
had for me!

제인, 네가 준 신부 선물 어떻게 감사를 해야 할지 모르겠어.

Mary: What does bridal shower mean?

신부 선물이 무슨 뜻이니?

Susie: Bridal showers are given by _____ friends of the bride to be
as a sort of dowry. The shower gifts are usually the domestic
variety, such as linens and kitchen utensils.

결혼축하 선물 증정파티는 예비 신부의 친한 친구들이 열어
주는 일종의 혼수 마련 잔치야. 보통 이 잔치의 선물들은 식

탁보나 주방 기구와 같은 다양한 가정용품들이야.

Jane: My _____! You really got some lovely gifts. Those kitchen utensils will sure come in handy.

천만에. 정말 멋진 선물들을 받았구나. 주방 기구들은 쓸모가 있을 거야.

Susie: Well. I guess I'll now have to learn how to _____.

그래 이제는 내가 요리하는 법을 배워야겠네.

■ Words & Phrases

bridal shower: 여성의 결혼 전 여자 친구들이 선물을 가지고 모이는 축하파티
close: 가까운
a sort of: 일종의
dowry: 결혼지참금
domestic: 가사의
variety: 잡동사니, 다양한 물건
such as: ~같은
utensil: 용구, 그릇
handy: 편리한
come in handy: 쓸모가 있다, 편리하다

■ Grammatical Points

I can't thank you enough for the bridal shower you had for me!

: I can't thank you enough는 '뭐라고 감사의 말을 할지 모르겠다'의 뜻이고 for 뒤에는 이유가 온다. the bridal shower (which) you had for me에서 목적격 관계대명사 which가 생략되었고 you had for me는 the bridal shower를 수식한다.

Bridal showers are given by close friends of the bride to be as a sort of dowry.

: are given은 수동태 문장이다. bride to be는 '신부가 될'의 뜻이고 as는 '~로서'이다. 능동태는 Close friends of the bride to be give bridal showers as a sort of dowry.

how to cook

: 요리하는 법

07 Cancer survival rate up

암 생존율 개선

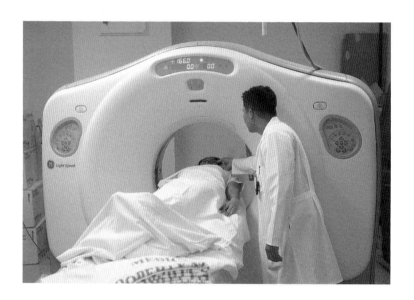

Reading Comprehension

The survival rate for cancer patients has increased significantly over the past five years, ① a positive sign for those trying to overcome the disease. The rate reached 64.1 percent between 2006 and 2012, up from 53.7 percent between 2001 and 2005, and 44 percent between 1996 and 2000. For rate of cancer occurrence has increased by 3.5 percent on the average every year since 1996-5.6 percent for women and 1.6 percent for men. For the average Korean, if they live until 81, the probability of suffering from cancer was 36.4 percent. Two out of five men and one out of three women are likely to be afflicted with the disease.

② The rate of cancer occurrence in Korea was higher than the global standard, standing at 282.3 people out of 100,000 compared with the OECD average of 256.5. ③ However, the numbers were lower than those of the United States(300.2) and Canada(296.6).

지난 5년간 암환자의 생존율이 상당히 높아짐으로써 암을 극복하려는 사람들에게 긍정적인 조짐이다. 생존율은 2006년에서 2012년에 64.1퍼센트로 2001에서 2005년의 53.7퍼센트 1996년에서 2000년의 44퍼센트보다 높았다. 1999년 이후 매년 암 발생 증가율은 연평균 3.5%였으며-여성 5.6%이고 남성 1.6%이다. 한국 국민의 평균 81세까지 산다면 암 발생률은 36.4%이고 남성은 5명 중 2명, 여성은 3명 중 1명이 암에 걸리기 쉽다. 한국에서 암 발생률은 인구 10만 명당 282.3명으로, 미국(300.2명), 캐나다(296.6명)보다는 낮았으나 경제협력기구(OECD) 평균(256.5명)보다는 높았다.

■ Words & Phrases

survival rate: 생존율
cancer patient: 암환자
significantly: 의미 있게, 중요하게
positive: 긍정적인
overcome: 극복하다
disease: 병, 질병
reach: ~에 이르다, ~에 달하다, 도달하다, 미치다
on the average: (양, 비율 따위가) 평균~
rate: 비율
probability: 가능성
occurrence: 발생
suffer from: ~을 겪다
be likely to: ~일 것 같다, 아마~인
be afflicted with: ~로 괴롭히다
global standard: 국제적인 기준
compared with: ~와 비교해서

■ Grammatical Points

① a positive sign for those trying to overcome the disease.

: a positive sign for those (who are) trying to overcome the disease. '주격 관계대명사 who+be 동사'가 생략되었다. those 는 people의 뜻이다.

② The rate of cancer occurrence in Korea was higher than the global standard, standing at 282.3 people out of 100,000 compared with the OECD average of 256.5.

: standing은 분사구문으로 'and the rate of cancer occurrence

in Korea stands~'에서 접속사 and와 주어를 생략하고 동사를 standing으로 바꾸어 만든 분사구문 형태이다. compared with the OECD average of 256.5도 분사구문이다. 'when the rate of cancer occurrence in Korea is compared with~'에서 when 과 주어가 생략하고 동사를 being compared로 바꾼 후 being 을 생략한 것이다.

③ **However, the numbers were lower than those of the United States(300.2) and Canada(296.6).**

: those는 앞의 말의 반복을 피하기 위한 대명사로서 the numbers를 대신한 것이다.

Speaking Practice

Doctor: Well, Mrs. Pak, I've _____ my examination and I'm happy to say it's nothing _____.

자, 박 여사님, 진찰이 끝났습니다. 증상이 전혀 심하지 않아 다행입니다.

Mrs. Pak: Don't you think you should _____ X-rays?

엑스레이를 찍어야 하지 않을까요?

Doctor: I don't think X-rays will be _____ for this illness.

이 병에는 엑스레이를 찍을 필요가 없다고 생각합니다.

Mrs. Pak: It's a _____ disease, isn't it?

전염병이죠?

Doctor: You have the _____.

감기입니다.

Mrs. Pak: Can I be _____ easily?

쉽게 치료될 수 있을까요?

Doctor: Yes, You listen to my advice and I'm certain you'll be fine.

네, 제 말씀대로 하시면 확실히 나으실 겁니다.

Mrs. Pak: What _____ I do?

무엇을 해야 할까요?

Doctor: _____ this medicine _____ four hours and get _____ of

rest. There's nothing to worry _____.

네 시간마다 이 약을 드시고 충분한 휴식을 취하세요. 걱

정하실 것 없습니다.

■ Words & Phrases

complete: ~을 끝내다
contagious: 전염성의
flu: 유행성 감기
take: (사진을) 찍다, (약을) 먹다
cure: 치료하다
every four hours: 네 시간에 한 번
plenty of: 많은
rest: 휴식

it's nothing serious

: anything, something, everything, nothing과 같이 '－thing'으로 끝나는 명사는 형용사가 앞이 아니고 뒤에서 수식한다.

There's nothing to worry about.

: to worry about은 앞에 있는 nothing을 수식하는 to 부정사의 형용사적 용법으로 쓰였다.

Unit

08 Coffee

커피

Reading Comprehension

① It is a well-known fact that the coffee tree, though of African origin, was first cultivated in the southwestern corner of the Arabian Peninsula. When coffee was first introduced into Europe in the 16th century, there were many arguments for and against its use. Some people went so far as to claim that coffee was poison, and said that,

② if it were drunk over a long period, it would kill a person. Today, however, coffee is enjoyed almost all over the world.

커피는 아프리카가 원산지이지만 아라비아 반도의 남서부 끝자락에서 처음 재배되었다. 커피가 16세기 처음 유럽에 소개되었을 때 커피의 사용에 대한 많은 찬반 논쟁이 있었다. 몇몇 사람들은 커피가 독이라고 주장하기까지 이르렀으며 만약에 장기간 마신다면 사람을 죽게까지 할 거라고 말했다. 그러나 오늘날 커피는 거의 전 세계에 걸쳐 애용되고 있다.

■ Words & Phrases

well-known: 유명한
though: ~일지라도
origin: 근원, 태생
cultivate: 재배하다
southwestern: 남서의
Arabian Peninsula: 아라비아 반도, 아라비아 반도는 아시아와 아프리카를 잇는 서아시아의 사막으로 이루어진 반도로 중동의 중심을 이룬다. 아시아 남서부에 있는 세계 최대의 반도이다. 사막성 기후이며 5~10월에는 고온다습하다.
argument: 논쟁
for and against: 찬성과 반대
use: 사용
so far as=as far as: ~까지
claim: 주장하다
poison: 독, 독약

■ Grammatical Points

① **It is a well-known fact that …**

: it은 가주어, that 이하는 진주어이다.

② **if it were drunk over a long period, it would kill a person.**

: 가정법 과거의 문장이다.

※ **가정법 과거: 현재의 사실에 반대되는 것을 가정할 때**

(조건절) …한다면	(귀결절) ~ 하겠는데(할 수 있을 텐데)
if …were, 혹은 과거형	…would, should, could, might+원형

· 가정법 과거의 조건절의 be 동사는 인칭에 관계없이 were를 쓰는 것이 원칙이지만 구어체에서는 1, 3인칭의 경우 was도 많이 쓰인다.
　e.g. If I were [was]rich, I could buy a car.
　　　(내가 부자라면 차를 살 수 있겠는데.)
　　　=As I am not rich, I cannot buy a car.
　　　(나는 부자가 아니기 때문에 차를 살 수 없다.)

　　　If I knew her phone number, I could call her.
　　　(내가 그녀의 전화번호를 안다면 전화할 수 있을 텐데.)
　　　=As I don't know her phone number, I cannot call her.
　　　(나는 그녀의 전화번호를 알 수 없기 때문에 그녀에게 전화할 수가 없다.)

Speaking Practice

A: How _____ some coffee?

커피 어때?

B: That's a great idea. I feel dead _____.

좋은 생각이야. 피곤해 죽겠어.

A: Where _____ we go?

어디 갈까?

B: Oh, we don't have to go anywhere. There is a coffee _____
around that corner.

아, 우리 어디 갈 필요 없어. 저 모퉁이를 돌면 커피 자판기가
있거든.

A: Okay, Here is a thousand won.

좋아, 여기 1,000원이 있어.

B: Oh, no! This machine is out of _____. And I can't get my
   money _____.

   오, 이런! 이 기계가 고장이 났네. 그리고 돈이 나오지도 않아.

A: _____ it. Let's go to the coffee shop _____ the street.

   잊어버려. 길 건너 커피숍으로 가자.

■ Words & Phrases
dead: (죽은 것처럼 지쳐서 축 늘어진)
out of order: 고장 난
get back: 도로 찾다
forget: 잊다
across: ~을 가로질러

■ Grammatical Points

How about some coffee?

: How about~?은 '~하는 것은 어때?'의 의미로 명사나 동명사
가 뒤에 온다.

Where shall we go?

: shall we~?는 '우리~할까요?'의 뜻이다.

Unit

09 Trading goods and services
재화와 서비스

Reading Comprehension

Trade began before history was recorded. ① Things or article that you trade are called goods. Services, such as building a house or cutting someone's hair, can be traded too. The exchange of goods or services for other goods or services is called the barter system.

Trade became easier when money was invented. The first money used was probably shells, stones, or beads. Later people began to use metal bars and coins. ② Then paper money was invented, and it made trading even easier. Paper bills are easier to carry than large amounts of metal or coins.

Everything we produce and trade—food, manufactured goods, labor, and services—has a money value. ③ The value of goods and services depends on how much money people are willing to pay for them.

거래는 역사가 기록되기도 전에 시작되었다. 당신이 교환하는 물건들이나 물품들을 상품이라 부른다. 집을 짓거나 머리카락을 자르는 일과 같은 서비스(용역)들 역시 교환될 수 있었다. 상품들과 용역들을 다른 상품과 용역들로 교환하는 것을 물물 교환제라고 부른다.

돈이 발명되자 거래는 좀 더 용이해졌다. 최초로 사용된 돈을 아마도 조가비나 돌멩이 혹은 구슬들이었을 것이다. 이후에 사람들은 금속 막대기나 동전을 사용하기 시작했다. 그리고 나서야 지폐가 발명되었고, 그로 인해 교역은 훨씬 쉬워졌다. 지폐는 많은 양의 금속이나 동전들보다 운반하기가 용이하다.

우리가 생산하고 거래하는 모든 것들-음식, 제조품, 노동 그리고 용역들-은 금전상의 가치를 지닌다. 상품과 용역의 가치는 사람들이 그것들을 얻기 위하여 얼마만큼의 돈을 지불하고자 하는가에 달려 있다.

■ **Words & Phrases**

trade: 거래, 무역
goods: 상품
exchange: 교환하다
barter: 물물 교환
invent: 발명하다
shell: 조가비, 껍데기
bead: 유리알, 구슬
metal bar: 금속 막대
bill: 지폐
value: 가치
depend on: ~에 달려 있다
be willing to: 기꺼이~ 하는

■ **Grammatical Points**

① **Things or article that you trade are called goods.**

  : that은 주격 관계대명사로서 you trade가 things or article를 수식하여 '당신들이 거래하는 물건이나 물품'으로 해석된다. 또한 동사 are called는 수동태로서 '불리어지다'라는 뜻이다.

② **Then paper money was invented, and it made trading even easier.**

  : it은 paper money이고 even은 비교급 easier를 수식해서 강조를 위한 '훨씬'이라는 뜻이다.

③ **The value of goods and services depends on how much money people are willing to pay for them.**

  : how much money people are willing to pay for them은 간접의문문으로 '의문사+주어+동사'의 어순이다.

Speaking Practice

A: What kind of shoes would you _____, ma'am? We have various _____ of shoes. Would you like some dress shoes or just casual_____?

어떤 종류의 신발을 찾으시나요, 부인? 우리는 다양한 신발을 가지고 있습니다. 정장용 신발인가요, 아니면 캐주얼 신발인가요?

B: Well, I'm looking _____ some walking shoes. Would suede shoes be good for that?

음, 전 보행용 신발을 찾고 있었어요. 스웨이드 가공 처리된 신발이 좋나요?

A: Yes, they would, but perhaps calfskin shoes would be the _____.

예, 그렇지요. 하지만 그래도 소가죽이 가장 좋을 거예요.

B: Okay. Could you show me several _____ of each kind?

좋아요. 각 종류로 몇 켤레 보여주시겠어요?

A: Certainly, ma'am. What' your size, please?

물론이죠, 부인. 사이즈가 어떻게 되시나요?

B: Seven and a half.

7과 1/2이요.

A: Here's a pair in your size. They are very good for the price.

여기 부인 사이즈입니다. 가격도 매우 저렴합니다.

B: Could I _____them on?

신어 봐도 될까요?

A: Certainly⋯. How do they _____?

물론이죠⋯. 느낌이 어떠세요?

B: Well, they're a little _____.

음, 약간 끼는군요.

■ Grammatical Points

Could you show me several pairs of each kind?

: show는 수여동사로 'show+간접목적어(사람)+직접목적어(사물)'
의 구문으로 쓰인다.

Could I try them on?

: 목적어 them이 대명사이므로 try와 on 사이에 와야 한다.
try on them (x)

10 Koreans spending more on luxury goods for kids

한국인들 아동 럭셔리 상품 구매 늘어

Reading Comprehension

Now is the so-called era of "eight pockets for one mouth." Due to a falling birthrate, almost eight people—parents, grandparents, aunts and uncles—feed the family's only child. According to the latest OECD data, Korea's birthrate was 1, 3 children per woman in 2012. It was the second lowest figure among 27 member nations only behind Portugal.

① Having a child is no longer obligation but an issue of choice. If a couple has chosen to have one, they are willing to spend big on the child. ② Propelled by the nations's famous fever for luxury goods, related markets have been soaring recently.

Junior labels of European luxury fashion houses like Burberry, Gucci and Armani have been piling into Korea.

지금은 '8명이 1명을 키우는 시대'다. 저출산으로 부모, 조부모, 숙부, 숙모 등 8명 정도가 집안의 유일무이한 어린이를 키우고 있다는 뜻이다. 최신 OECD 자료에 따르면 한국의 출산율은 2012년 여성 1명당 1.3명이었다. 이는 27개 회원국 중 최하위인 포르투갈 다음으로 낮은 수치였다.

자식을 낳는다는 것은 더 이상 의무가 아니라 선택의 문제가 됐다. 만약 부부가 자식을 낳기로 했다면 자식에 많은 돈을 기꺼이 쓸 준비가 됐다는 말이다. 사치품을 선호하는 국민 성향 덕분에 관련 시장은 최근 호황을 맞았다.

버버리, 구찌, 아르마니 같은 유럽의 럭셔리 패션 업체들의 어린이용 상표들이 한국에 몰려들고 있다.

■ Words & Phrases

so-called: 소위
era: 시대
due to: ～때문에
falling: 떨어지는, 감소하는
birthrate: 출산율
aunt: 숙모, 이모
uncle: 삼촌, 외삼촌
feed: 먹이다, 먹여 살리다
according to: ～에 따르면
the latest: 최근의
per: ～마다
figure: 숫자, 모양, 인물
have a child: 자식을 낳다
no longer: 더 이상～아니다
obligation: 의무
issue of choice: 선택의 문제
fever: 열기, 과열
propel: 추진하다
luxury goods: 사치품
surge: 급등하다, 고조되다
junior: 어린이의
label: 라벨, 상표
pile into: 밀려 들어오다

■ Grammatical Points

① **Having a child is no longer obligation**

: 주어는 having a child로 동명사 주어이며 동명사 주어는 단
수 취급하므로 단수 동사인 is가 사용되었다.

② **Propelled by the nations's famous fever for luxury goods, related markets have been soaring recently.**

: 분사구문으로서 being이 생략되었다.

=As related markets are propelled by the nations's famous fever for luxury goods, related markets have been soaring recently의 문장에서 접속사 as를 지우고 주절의 주어와 같은 related markets를 지우고 나면 Being propelled by~의 분사구문이 된다. 그런데 수동태의 분사구문에서 being은 생략되는 경우가 많다.

Speaking Practice

A: How do I look ___ this jacket?

이 재킷 입은 모습이 어떻게 보여요?

B: You _____ very good. I think this blue jacket _____ you better than the black ____.

멋져 보입니다. 이 파란 재킷이 까만 재킷보다 더 잘 어울린다고 생각됩니다.

A: I think so, too. So how much is this jacket?

저도 그렇게 생각합니다. 이 재킷은 얼마입니까?

B: Its _____ price is $200, but it's 10% ____ right now.

정가는 200불인데 지금은 10% 할인입니다.

A: That sounds good. Okay, I'll buy this jacket.

좋군요. 이 재킷을 사겠어요.

B: How would you like to ____?

어떻게 계산하시겠어요?

A: My credit card. Here is the⋯. Oh, where's my _____?

신용카드로요. 여기⋯. 어, 내 지갑이 어디 갔지?

B: Is something wrong?

무슨 문제가 생겼나요?

A: I'm sorry, but I think I ____ my wallet in the car. I have to
   go back to the parking ___.

미안합니다. 지갑을 자동차에 두고 온 것 같습니다. 주차장에
다시 가야 합니다.

B: No problem. It often happens to _____.

괜찮습니다. 고객들에게 종종 일어나는 일입니다.

■ Words & Phrases

look: 보이다
suit: 어울리다
regular price: 보통 가격
happens to: ~에 일어나다
customer: 고객

■ Grammatical Points

How do I look in this jacket?

: in은 (착용) 입고, 쓰고, 신고의 의미이다.

I think this blue jacket suits you better than the black one.

: one은 jacket을 대신한 대명사이다.

that sounds good

: sound는 2형식 문장에서 쓰이는 동사로 '～처럼 들리다'의 뜻
이다. sound 뒤에는 형용사가 쓰인다. 이처럼 주격보어가 필요한
불완전 자동사에는 be, smell, look, turn, become, grow 등이 있다.

Unit

11 Singing is Good for Your Health

노래 부르는 것은 건강에 좋아

Reading Comprehension

Music makes us happy. ① Listening to good music helps us relax and relieve stress. ② This is why people all over the world love music. Did you know that singing is actually good for your health? It will help you in many surprising ways.

Singing can lower your blood pressure and reduce pain. ③ Singing your favorite songs helps you relax and reminds you of happy time. It also helps you breathe easier. ④ If you are suffering from respiratory problems, singing just twice a week could make breathing feel easier.

And ⑤ singing can increase your immunity, reduce stress, and ease anxiety. Some people even say that singing helped fix their snoring problems.

음악은 우리를 행복하게 만들어줍니다. 좋은 음악을 들으면 긴장을 풀고 스트레스를 해소하는 데 도움이 됩니다. 그래서 전 세계 사람들이 음악을 좋아하는 것입니다. 노래를 부르는 것이 실제로 건강에 좋다는 것을 아십니까? 그것은 많은 놀라운 면에서 당신을 도울 것입니다.

노래는 당신의 혈압을 낮추어 주고 고통을 줄여 줍니다. 당신이 좋아하는 노래를 부르는 것은 긴장을 풀고 행복한 시절을 기억하게 하는 데 도움이 됩니다. 만약 호흡기 질환을 앓고 있다면, 일주일에 두 차례 노래를 부르는 것만으로도 호흡을 더 쉽게 할 수 있습니다.

그리고 노래는 면역력을 증가시키고, 스트레스를 줄이며, 근심 걱정을 완화시킬 수 있습니다. 어떤 사람들은 심지어 노래가 코를 고는 문제도 고치는 데 도움이 되었다고 말하기도 합니다.

relieve: 제거하다, 풀어주다
relieve stress: 스트레스를 풀다
this is why: 이것이~의 이유다
even if: ~일지라도
be good at: ~에 잘하다
in many ways: 많은 방식(면)에서
blood pressure: 혈압
reduce: 줄이다
relax: 완화하다, 쉬게 하다
remind A of B: A에게 B를 상기시키다
breathe: 호흡하다
suffer from: 겪다, 고통받다
respiratory: 호흡 기간의, 호흡 작용의
immunity: 면역
reduce: 줄이다
ease: 완화하다, 경감하다
anxiety: 근심, 걱정
fix: 고치다
snore: 코를 골다

■ Grammatical Points

사역동사

① Listening to good music <u>helps</u> <u>us</u> <u>relax and relieve</u> stress.

: 사역동사+사람+(to) 동사

사람이~(동사)하는 것을 돕다

(좋은 음악을 듣는 것은 우리가 긴장을 풀고 스트레스를 해소하는 것을 돕는다.)

② **This is why people all over the world love music.**

: 'this is why'는 '이것이~이유이다'의 뜻이다.

This is why I came.

(이것이 내가 온 이유다.)

③ **Singing your favorite songs helps you relax and reminds you of happy time.**

: 'help+사람+(to) relax'은 '사람이 relax하는 것을 돕다'의 뜻이다. 이 문장에서 주어는 singing your favorite songs이고 동사는 helps와 reminds이다. 'remind A of B'는 'A에게 B 생각나게 하다'의 뜻이다.

④ **If you are suffering from respiratory problems, singing just twice a week could make breathing feel easier.**

: '사역동사 make, let, have+목적어+동사의 원형'이다.

일주일에 단지 두 번을 노래하는 것은 호흡하는 것이 쉽게 느껴지게 만든다.

⑤ **singing can increase your immunity, reduce stress, and ease anxiety.**

: 문장에서 주어는 singing이고, 동사는 increase, reduce, ease이다.

Speaking Practice

A: You look _____. What _____?

너 창백해 보인다. 무슨 일이니?

B: I didn't sleep a _____ last night.

지난밤에 한잠도 못 잤어.

A: Did you have something on your mind? You look so _____!

마음에 걸리는 거라도 있니? 걱정스러워 보여.

B: Well, I'm _____ a lot of pressure. My boss is very _____. He
_____ me three projects. Now the _____ are near and I still
haven't finished all of my projects.

음, 난 압박감을 느끼고 있어. 사장이 상당히 추진력이 강해. 그
가 나에게 세 개의 과제를 맡겼어. 이제 최종 기한이 다가오는
데 난 아직 모든 과제를 끝내지 못했어.

A: Is there _____ I can do to help you?

내가 도와줄 일이 있을까?

B: Well, I guess no one can help me _____ myself. For the
moment, I just need someone to talk to so that I can _____
my stress.

글쎄, 난 내 자신 외에는 아무도 날 도울 수 없다고 생각해. 나
는 단지 스트레스를 풀 수 있도록 잠시 동안이라도 이야기할
사람이 필요해.

■ Words & Phrases

a wink: 짧은 잠
concerned: 근심스러운, 걱정하는
under a lot of pressure: 많은 압박감을 느끼는
pushy: 추진력이 강한
assign: 할당하다
deadline: 마감 시간
relieve stress: 스트레스를 풀다

■ Grammatical Points

Is there anything I can do to help you?

: Is there anything (that) I can do to help you? 관계대명사 that 의 목적격이 생략되어 있다.

I guess no one can help me but myself.

: but은 '~을 제하고는, ~외에는'의 뜻이다. I guess (that) no one can help me but myself에서는 접속사 that이 생략되어 있다.

I just need someone to talk to so that I can relieve my stress.

: to talk to가 someone을 수식한다. so that 주어 can은 '주어가~ 할 수 있도록'의 뜻이다.

Unit

12 No time for Exercise?

운동할 시간이 없나요?

Reading Comprehension

① The moment your alarm goes off at six, another busy day begins as usual. You leave home at eight and spend many hours at school. ② You do homework, take lessons, and do a variety of other things a typical college student is supposed to do everyday. It may be past midnight when you go to bed. Throughout the day, you don't engage in much physical activity. In other words, you don't exercise. From time to time you think that you need some exercise, but don't you always tell yourself that you have no time for it?

If you think you have no time to exercise, think again. You can take half an hour everyday, and do some kind of physical activity. Wash windows or floors, play basketball, bicycle, dance, swim, jump rope, run, or even walk the stairs! ③ It doesn't matter what physical activity you do.

자명종이 6시에 울리자마자 평소와 같이 또 다른 날이 시작된다. 너는 8시에 집을 나와 학교에서 많은 시간을 보낸다. 숙제를 하고 수업을 듣고 전형적인 대학생들이 매일 하는 다양한 많은 일들을 한다. 네가 잠자리에 들 때면 자정이 넘을 수 있다. 하루 종일 너는 많은 육체적 활동에 관여하지 못한다. 즉 너는 운동을 하지 않는다. 때때로 너는 네가 운동이 좀 필요하다고 생각한다. 그러나 자신에게 운동을 할 시간이 없다고 언제나 말하지 않는가?

만약에 운동할 시간이 없다고 생각한다면, 다시 생각해 봐라. 너는 매일 30분 시간을 낼 수 있다. 그리고 일종의 육체 활동을 해라. 창문이나 마루를 닦아라, 농구, 자전거 춤, 수영, 줄넘기 혹은 계단을 올라라. 무슨 육체적 활동을 하는가는 중요하지 않다.

the moment (that): ~하자마자
go off: (자명종이) 울리다, 갑자기~ 하다
as usual: 평소와 같이
a variety of: 다양한, 다채로운 (복수명사가 온다)
typical: 전형적인, 대표적인
be supposed to~: ~하도록 되어 있다
throughout: ~동안 내내, 처음부터 끝까지
engage in: ~에 관여하다,~에 종사하다
from time to time: 때때로, 가끔
physical: 신체의, 육체의
activity: 활동, 행위
in other words: 바꾸어 말하자면, 즉
floor: 마룻바닥
jump rope: 줄넘기
stair: 계단
matter: 중요하다

■ Grammatical Points

① The moment your alarm goes off at six, another busy day begins as usual.

: your alarm goes off at six가 the moment를 수식한다. '너의 알람시계가 6시에 울리는 순간에'라는 뜻이다.

② You do homework, take lessons, and do a variety of other things a typical college student is supposed to do everyday.

: 목적격 관계대명사 that이 생략되어 있고 a typical college student is supposed to do everyday가 things를 수식한다.

③ **It doesn't matter what physical activity you do.**

: matter는 동사로 중요하다의 뜻이다. it은 가주어이고 진주어는 what physical activity you do로서 '무슨 육체적 활동을 하는 것은 중요하지 않다'라는 뜻이다.

Speaking Practice

A: I have no _____ and I'm tired all the time. What's _____
with me, doctor?

전 기운이 없고 늘 피곤해요. 의사 선생님, 뭐가 문제지요?

B: Are you eating nutritious meals three _____ a day?

하루에 세 번씩 영양가 있는 식사를 하시나요?

A: Well, not really. I'm so busy that I often only have a quick
_____ between classes.

그렇지 못해요. 너무 바빠서 종종 수업 시간 사이에 급히 간식
을 먹는 정도예요.

B: I see. And what about _____ activity?

그렇군요. 그럼 운동은 좀 합니까?

A: As I said, I'm busy. I've got no time.

말씀드린 것처럼 저는 바빠요. 시간이 없어요.

B: You will simply have to take time _____ from your schedule to eat good meals and to exercise. _____, you'll end up in serious trouble.

일과 중에 시간을 내서 식사를 잘하고, 운동을 해야 할 거예요. 그렇지 않으면 나중에 심각한 문제가 생길 테니까요.

■ Words & Phrases

energy: 기운
nutritious: 영양이 있는
snack: 간식
take time off: 시간을 떼놓다
otherwise: 만약 그렇지 않으면
end up: 마지막에는~ 이 되다

■ Grammatical Points

You will simply have to take time off from your schedule to eat good meals and to exercise.

: to eat good meals and to exercise는 to 부정사의 부사적 용법으로서 '좋은 식사를 하고 운동을 하기 위하여'의 뜻이다.

Otherwise, you'll end up in serious trouble.

: otherwise는 '만약 그렇지 않다면'의 뜻이다.

My parents lent me the money. Otherwise, I couldn't have afforded the trip. (우리 부모님이 내게 그 돈을 빌려주셨다. 안 그랬으면 내가 그 여행을 할 형편이 안 되었을 것이다.)

Unit

13 "Trick or Treat" on Halloween

할로인 날의 "사탕 줄래요, 골탕 먹을래요"

Reading Comprehension

Halloween falls on October 31. ① It is believed that on this day, ghosts, spirits, and witches come out to harm people. In order to scare the evil spirits away, people place scary decoration such as black cats, skeletons, and ghosts in front of their homes. ② Children dressed in masks and colorful costumes go from door to door saying "trick or treat", and people give them candy, cookies, fruit, or money.

할로윈 날은 10월 31일이다. 유령들과 영혼들 그리고 마녀들이 사람들에게 해를 끼치려고 이날 나오는 것으로 믿어지고 있다. 나쁜 영혼들을 겁주어 쫓게 하기 위해 사람들은 자신들의 집 앞에 검은 고양이, 해골, 유령과 같은 무시무시한 장식들을 놓아둔다. 가면과 화려한 의상을 입은 아이들은 "사탕 줄래요, 골탕 먹을래요" 하고 외치며 이 집 저 집으로 다니고 사람들은 아이들에게 사탕이나, 과자 과일이나 돈을 준다.

■ Words & Phrases

fall on: (휴일 따위가, ~ 이) 오다
ghost: 유령
harm: 해를 입히다
scare: 겁나게 하다, 위협하다
evil spirits: 악령
place: 놓다
scary: 무서운, 무시무시한
such as: ~ 같은
skeleton: 해골
costume: 복장, 옷차림

■ Grammatical Points

① **It is believed that on this day, ghosts, spirits, and witches come out to harm people.**

: =They believe that on this day, ghosts, spirits, and witches come out to harm people의 수동태형이다.

② **Children (who are) dressed in masks and colorful costumes…**

: 주격 관계대명사 who+be 동사가 생략. dressed in masks and colorful costumes가 children을 수식한다.

■ Note

jack-o'lantern: (할로윈에 쓰는) 호박 초롱
할로윈 데이에 누런 호박의 속을 파고 껍질에 무서운 얼굴을 새긴 다음 그 안에 촛불을 넣은 호박 초롱을 jack-o'lantern이라고 부른다. 전설에 의하며 이 명칭은 인색하고 야비해서 죽어서 천국에도 지옥에도 가지 못한 Jack이란 아일랜드 노인으로부터 유래되었다고 한다.

prank: 못된 장난
할로윈 데이에 사람들은 악의 없는 장난을 많이 치는데, 대표적인 것으로는 이웃집이나 차에 달걀을 던지는 egging과 이웃집이나 나무를 밤새 휴지로 감싸는 toilet papering 등이 있다.

Trick or treat?: 장난을 칠까요, 먹을 것을 줄래요?
할로윈에 아이들이 집집마다 다니며 문 밖에서 Trick or treat?이라고 외치면, 주부들이 아이들이 장난치지 않도록 사탕을 준다.

Speaking Practice

A: Were you _____ that I dressed up? It's Halloween. (October 31)

내가 분장을 해서 놀랐지? 오늘이 10월 31일 할로인 축제날이거든.

B: Halloween?

할로윈이라고?

A: Yes, we usually dress up as ghosts and monsters and go round to people's houses asking, "_____ or_____." Can you figure out what I _____?

응. 우리는 귀신이나 괴물의 모습으로 분장하고 집집마다 돌아 다니면서 '과자를 주지 않으면 장난을 칠 거예요'라고 말하지. 내가 하는 말 이해할 수 있겠니?

B: Yes, a little. What ___ the children do not get a treat?

그래. 약간은 이해할 수 있어. 만일 아이들이 과자를 받지 못하면 어떻게 되지?

A: They usually _____ the windows. It's a _____.

그들은 보통 유리창에 비누칠을 해. 그게 장난이야.

B: That's ___ ! Do they have any parties, too?

그거 재미있구나! 아이들은 파티도 하니?

A: Of course. During the party they usually play games such as getting apples out of water using only their mouth.

물론이지. 파티를 여는 동안 그들은 보통 입만 사용하여 물에서 사과를 꺼내는 것 같은 게임을 하지.

■ Words & Phrases

dress up: 분장하다, 야단스럽게 차려입다
figure out: 이해하다=understand
Trick or treat!: 과자를 주지 않으면 장난을 칠 거예요
(미국에서 Halloween 때 아이들이 집집마다 돌아다니면서 '과자를 주지 않으면 장난을 칠 테야' 하고 으름장을 놓은 말)
what if~?: ~하면 어찌 되는가?
soap the window: 비누로 창문을 문지르다
get A out of B: B에서 A를 꺼내다

■ Grammatical Points

Can you figure out what I mean?

: figure out의 목적어인 what I mean은 간접의문문이다.

※ **간접의문문**

간접의문문은 의문문이 문장의 일부로 되어 있는 경우인데, 의문사와 접속사로 이끌려 [주어+동사]의 어순을 갖는다. 의문사가 있는 경우에는 그 의문사를 그대로 쓰고, 의문사가 없을 때는 if나 whether를 써서 두 글을 연결한다.
I know + who is he → I know who he is. (나는 그가 누군지 안다.)
Do you know who she is? (그녀가 누구인지 아니?)
Do you know? + Is he a doctor?
→ Do you know if (or whether) he is a doctor?

‖ 주의 ‖ think, believe, imagine, guess, suppose 등의 동사가 쓰일 때는 의문사가 문장의 맨 앞에 놓인다.
Do you think + Who is he?
→ Who do you think he is? (너는 그가 누구라고 생각하니?)

Sunlight gives us more benefits than harm

태양은 우리에게 해로움보다는 혜택을 더 많이 준다

Reading Comprehension

Many experts believe that ① sunlight gives us more benefits than harm. It is because ② getting enough sunlight is very important for all living creatures.

First, plants need sunlight to make their "photosynthesis." It is a process in which plants change light energy from the sun into sugar.

③ If it were not for sunlight, plants would disappear for lack of food.

Second, sunlight can be used to treat depression in people. It is because sunlight causes our brain to produce a good mood chemical. So doctors advise depressed patients to get enough sunlight. Anytime you are down or upset, go out and spend some time in the sun. ④ It will make you feel a lot better.

많은 전문가들이 햇빛이 우리에게 해보다는 이익을 더 많이 주고 있다고 믿는다. 그것은 충분한 햇빛을 받는 것은 모든 살아 있는 생물들에게 매우 중요하기 때문이다.

먼저, 식물은 광합성을 만들기 위해 햇빛이 필요하다. 광합성은 식물이 태양으로부터의 빛 에너지를 포도당으로 변화시키는 과정이다. 만약에 햇빛이 없다면 식물들은 영향 부족으로 죽어버릴 것이다.

두 번째, 햇빛은 사람들의 우울을 치료하는 데 사용될 수 있다. 그것은 햇빛이 우리의 두뇌가 좋은 기운의 화학물질을 만들어내게 하기 때문이다. 그래서 의사들은 의기소침한 환자들에게 충분한 햇볕을 쬐도록 충고한다. 네가 화가 나거나 우울할 때 언제든지 밖으로 나가서 태양 아래에서 약간의 시간을 보내라. 그것은 너를 훨씬 기분이 좋아지게 만들 것이다.

■ Grammatical Points

① sunlight gives us more benefits

: give+간접목적어(…에게)+직접목적어(~을, 를)의 뜻을 가진 4형식 문장이다.

② getting enough sunlight is very important

: getting은 동명사로서 주어 역할을 한다.

③ If it were not for sunlight, plants would disappear for lack of food.

: If it were not for~, 주어 would(should, might, could)+동사원형

'~이 없다면'의 뜻의 가정법 과거이다. if it were not for 대신

에 without, but for를 쓸 수도 있다.

④ **It will make you feel**

: 사역동사는 '～하게 하다, 시키다'의 의미

make+목적어+원형 형태

Speaking Practice

A: You look so tired. What happened?

피곤해 보인다. 무슨 일 있어?

B: I only _____ for four hours last night.

어제 밤에 4시간밖에 못 잤거든.

A: Oh, that's too ____. Getting enough sleep is very _____.

이런, 너무 안됐다. 충분히 자는 건 정말 중요해.

B: If I don't get eight hours sleep, I'm tired the whole next day.

나는 하루에 8시간 자지 않으면 다음 날 하루 종일 피곤해.

A: What kept you _____ for so long? Exams?

왜 그렇게 잠을 못 잔거야? 시험 때문에?

B: You got it. I'm ___ stressed out about exams ___ I usually sleep for five hours these days. What should I do?

맞아. 요즘 시험 때문에 너무 스트레스 받아서 보통 5시간밖에 잘 수가 없어. 어쩌지?

A: You should learn how to _____.

긴장 푸는 법을 배워야 해.

■ Words & Phrases

whole: 전체의, 전(全)
awake: 잠을 자지 않고 있는, 눈을 뜨고 있는
how to relax: 긴장 푸는 법
these days: 요즈음

■ Grammatical Points

Getting enough sleep is very important

: getting enough sleep이 주어로서 getting은 동명사

I'm so stressed out about exams that I usually sleep for five hours these days

: 'so~ that…' 용법으로서 '매우~해서 …하다'의 뜻이다.

You should learn how to relax

: how to relax는 '긴장 푸는 법'이다.

Unit

15 Kimchi's nutritional qualities and the proper way to store it

김치의 영양가와 보존법

Reading Comprehension

Kimchi contains several key vitamins, ① including vitamin C. It also contains calcium and iron and gets a significant amount of vitamin E from its red pepper. In addition to that, ② Kimchi is high in fiber, which aids digestion and it contains only thirty-three calories per cup. All in all, it is fair to say that Kimchi is very good for the human body.

In order to keep the flavor and nutritional value of Kimchi, it is important to store it at a constant temperature, about five degrees Celsius. ③ If kept properly at this temperature, it will probably last four to six weeks. However, ④ one must also be careful to prevent air from entering the container, which will cause the kimchi to sour. ⑤ Traditional kimchi jars were wrapped in straw and then buried to maintain the best conditions for storing kimchi.

김치는 비타민 C를 비롯해서 필수 비타민 몇 가지를 함유하고 있습니다. 또한 칼슘과 철이 있고, 고추로부터 상당량의 비타민 E를 얻습니다. 그뿐만 아니라 김치는 소화를 돕는 섬유질이 풍부하고, 한 컵당 열량이 33칼로리밖에 되지 않습니다. 모든 걸 종합해 보면 김치는 사람 몸에 매우 이롭다고 분명히 말할 수 있습니다.

김치의 풍미와 영양학적인 가치를 유지하기 위해서는 일정한 온도, 약 섭씨 5도에서 보관하는 것이 중요합니다. 김치가 이 온도에서 적절히 보관되면, 4주에서 6주까지 맛이 지속될 겁니다. 그러나 공기가 김치통에 들어가지 않도록 조심해야 하는데, 만약 공기가 들어가게 되면 맛이 시어지기 때문입니다. 옛날 김칫독은 짚으로 싸서 땅에 묻어 두었는데, 이는 김치를 저장하기 위한 최적의 상태를 유지하기 위한 것이었습니다.

nutritional: 영양(상)의
nutritional quality: 영양가
proper: 적당한
store: 저장하다
contain: 포함하다
significant amount of: 상당량의
red pepper: 고추
in addition to~: ~에 더해서
key: 중요한
digestion: 소화
all in all: 종합하여 말하자면
flavor: 맛
constant: 계속되는
Celsius: 섭씨 (온도의 단위)
last: 지속하다
prevent A from B: A가 B 하는 것을 막다
preservation: 보관, 보존
store: 저장하다

■ Grammatical Points

① including vitamin C.

: =and it contains라는 문장에서 접속사 and와 it(Kimchi)를 생략하고 include에 ~ing을 붙여 분사구문을 만든다.

분사구문은 분사(현재분사, 과거분사)를 이용하여 부사절을 부사구로 만든 것을 말한다.

※ 분사구문

분사구문은 시간(when, while, as after, before), 이유(as, because, since), 조건(if, when), 양보(although) 등을 나타내는 접속사가 이끄는 부사절을 접속사와 주어 등을 생략하고, 동사를 분사형으로 바꾸어 나타낸 형태이다.

· 분사구문 만드는 법
① 부사절의 접속사를 생략한다.
② 주절의 주어와 부사절의 주어가 같을 때는 주어를 생략한다. 하지만 주어가 다를 경우 생략하지 않는다.
③ 남는 동사를 주절과 부사절의 시제가 같은 경우 '동사원형+ing'로 바꾸고, 부사절의 시제가 주절의 시제보다 앞서는 경우 'having+p.p.'로 바꾼다. 분사구문을 부정할 때는 분사 앞에 not 또는 never를 붙인다.
④ 수동태로 이루어진 문장에서 being, having been은 생략할 수 있다.

② Kimchi is high in fiber, which aids digestion and it contains only thirty…

: 관계대명사 which의 계속적 용법. which의 선행사는 앞 문장 Kimchi is high inifiber

③ If (it is) kept properly at this temperature,

: it is가 생략된 수동태 문장이다.

④ one must also be careful to prevent air from entering the container, which will cause the kimchi to sour.

: which는 관계대명사 계속적 용법으로서 해석은 앞에서 차례로 한다. cause A to B는 'A가 B 하도록 야기시키다'의 뜻이다.

⑤ Traditional kimchi jars were wrapped in straw and then buried to maintain the best conditions for storing kimchi.

: Traditional kimchi jars were wrapped in straw and then (were) buried에서 반복되는 동사(were)를 생략한 것이다. to maintain 은 '유지하기 위하여'라는 뜻으로 목적을 나타내는 to 부정사의 부사적 용법이다.

Speaking Practice

A: What's ___ dinner?

저녁으로 뭘 먹을까?

B: Let's get hamburgers.

햄버거 먹자.

A: We just ____ one yesterday. We can't eat hamburgers every day.

바로 어제도 먹었잖아. 매일 먹을 수는 없어.

B: But I don't want to ____ today.

하지만 오늘은 요리하기 싫단 말이야.

A: Look, eating ____ food is not good for our health if we eat it often.

이봐, 패스트푸드를 너무 자주 먹으면 건강에 해로워.

B: You mean that we're going to get sick if we don't stop ____ hamburgers? Can you really quit _____ fast food for ___ No more tomato sauce, cheese, and French fries for the rest of your life?

네 말은 우리가 햄버거 먹는 것을 중단하지 않으면 병에 걸릴 거라는 거니? 너는 정말 몸에 좋다는 이유로 패스트푸드를 먹지 않을 수 있어? 평생의 나머지 동안 더 이상의 토마토, 치즈, 프렌치프라이 없이?

A: I don't think I said that, exactly. But since we've just eaten junk food, for the time being we _____ have any more. That's what I ____.

정확히 그렇게는 말하지 않은 것 같은데. 하지만 내 말뜻은, 우리가 이미 그걸 먹었으니까 당분간은 또 먹으면 안 된다는 의미야.

B: Okay. then I'll cook today.

알았어. 그럼 오늘은 요리를 할게.

■ Words & Phrases

have: 먹다
get: 먹다
for good: 영원히
since: ~이므로, ~이기 때문에
for the time being: 당분간

eating junk food is not good for our health···

: 주어는 eating junk food로 동명사 주어는 단수로 취급하므로 단수 동사인 is를 사용했다.

Can you really quit eating fast food for good?

: 'quit+동명사'는 '~하는 것을 중단하다'라는 의미이다.

But since we've just eaten junk food, for the time being we shouldn't have any more.

: since는 '~이기 때문에'라는 뜻이다. shoudn't=should not의 줄임말로서 '~을 하지 말아야 한다'의 뜻이다.

That's what I mean.

: 관계대명사 what은 선행사를 포함하는 관계대명사로 문장에서 주어, 목적어, 보어로 쓰여 명사절을 이끌며, the thing(which)으로 대신할 수 있다. 이 문장에서는 보어로 쓰였고 '내가 의미하는 것'의 의미이다.

Fun Facts about Toilet Paper

화장지에 대한 재미있는 사실들

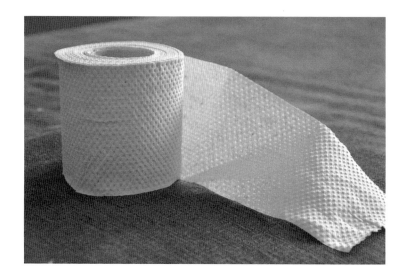

Reading Comprehension

People use toilet paper every day. ① As a matter of fact, it plays important roles in our daily lives. Can you imagine living without toilet paper? ② It would be really difficult to live without it. In fact, we use an average of 57 sheets of toilet paper a day! But how much do you know about toilet paper?

According to a survey, in an average household, the average roll of toilet paper lasts about five days. People use approximately 8 to 9 sheets of paper per toilet use.

A single tree can produce about 810 rolls of toilet paper. ③ It takes about 384 trees to make the toilet paper that one person uses within his or her lifetime. The average person uses 100 rolls of toilet paper per year. We should use toilet paper wisely to save trees.

사람들은 날마다 휴지를 사용합니다. 사실, 휴지는 우리의 일상생활에서 중요한 역할들을 하고 있습니다. 여러분은 화장지 없이 산다는 것을 상상할 수 있나요? 화장지 없이 산다는 것은 정말 어려울 거예요. 사실 우리는 하루에 평균적으로 57장의 화장지를 사용합니다. 하지만 당신은 화장지에 대해 얼마나 알고 있나요?

한 설문조사에 의하면, 보통의 가정에서 일반적인 화장지 한 롤은 약 5일 정도 간다고 합니다. 사람들은 한 번 화장실을 사용할 때마다 대략 8~9장의 휴지를 사용합니다.

나무 한 그루는 약 810롤의 화장지를 생산할 수 있습니다. 한 사람이 평생 동안 사용하는 화장지를 만들기 위해서는 약 384그루의 나무가 들어갑니다. 보통의 사람들은 100롤의 화장지를 사용합니다. 나무를 살리기 위해서는 화장지를 지혜롭게 사용해야 합니다.

■ **Words & Phrases**

toilet paper: 화장지
as a matter of fact: 사실상
play roles: 역할을 하다
daily lives: 일상생활
imagine: 상상하다
without: ~없이, ~이 없다면(가정법)
according to: ~에 따르면
survey: 조사
household: 집안, 가정, 세대
last: 지속되다
approximately: 약
sheet: 장
per: ~마다
produce: 생산하다
lifetime: 생애, 평생
save: 절약하다

■ Grammatical Points

① As a matter of fact, it plays important roles in our daily lives.

: play important roles는 중요한 역할을 하다의 뜻이다. lives는 life의 복수로서 삶, 생활의 뜻이다.

② It would be really difficult to live without it.

: 가정법 과거 문장이다. without은 '~이 없다면'의 뜻으로 if it were not for로 바꿔 쓸 수 있다.

③ It takes about 384 trees to make the toilet paper that one person uses within his or her lifetime.

: it은 가주어이고 진주어는 to make the toilet paper that one person uses within his or her lifetime이다. that은 목적격 관계 대명사로서 one person uses within his or her lifetime은 toilet paper를 수식한다.

Speaking Practice

A: I heard that you're _____ in environmentally friendly products.

난 네가 환경 친화 제품에 관심이 있다고 들었어.

B: Yes, I've been using those products to _____ the environment. Why do you ask?

맞아. 난 환경을 보존하기 위해 그런 제품을 사용해 왔어. 왜 물어보니?

A: I saw a really interesting documentary on new developments in technology last night.

난 어제 밤에 새로운 기술 발전에 대한 정말 흥미로운 다큐멘터리를 봤어.

B: I'm sorry I _____ that.

오, 내가 놓친 것이 아쉽다.

A: The one that really made me surprised was a prototype battery made from spinach.

나를 정말 놀라게 한 것은 시금치로 만들어진 건전지 초기 모델이야.

B: Spinach! That's a vegetable. I don't believe it.

시금치라고! 그건 채소야. 믿을 수 없어.

A: It's true. They can engineer spinach cells to _____ light into electricity to power something like a laptop computer.

정말이야. 그들은 시금치 세포들로 빛을 전기로 바꿔서 휴대용 컴퓨터 같은 것에 전력을 공급하도록 할 수 있어.

B: That's _____.

놀랍구나.

■ Words & Phrases

environmentally: 환경적으로
friendly: 친한
products: 제품
documentary: 다큐멘터리, 기록영화
prototype: 원형, 시작품
spinach: 시금치
cell: 세포
engineer: 처리하다
convert: 전환하다, 바꾸다
electricity: 전기
incredible: 엄청난, 대단한, 불가사의한

The one that really made me surprised was a prototype battery made from spinach.

: that really made me surprised가 the one을 수식하고 주어는 the one이다. 문장의 동사는 was이고 battery와 made 사이는 which was(주격 관계대명사+be 동사)가 생략되었다.

They can engineer spinach cells to convert light into electricity to power something like a laptop computer.

: engineer는 타동사로서 spinach cells가 목적어이고 to convert가 목적보어이다. to power는 부사적 용법으로 '전력을 공급하다'의 뜻이다.

Unit

17 Child Labor

어린이 노동

Reading Comprehension

① Child labor is one of the most serious problems faced by developing countries today. Children are forced to work long hours with dangerous machines. They are fed very little. Sometimes, they are even made to work as slaves and receive no pay at all.

A recent report by the United Nations said that much of the world's child labor goes toward producing basic things like coffee and cocoa. These and other products are traded widely and bring big profits to poor counties. ② The International Labor Organization(ILO) says that over 246 million children are being put to work worldwide. Of these, over 8 million are forced into sex trade.

Recently, it was discovered that many poor children in China are being forced into slave labor. Children as young as 8 are being kidnapped and put to work in factories and brickyards. The working conditions are often dangerous, and many children have been seriously hurt or killed.

어린이 노동은 오늘날 개발도상국들이 직면하고 있는 가장 심각한 문제 중의 하나이다. 어린이들은 위험한 기계를 다루는 장시간의 노동에 처해지고 있다. 그들은 먹는 것도 부족하다. 가끔 그들은 노예로 일을 하거나 전혀 임금을 받지 못하게 강요되고 있다.

UN의 최근 보고서에 의하면 세계 어린이 노동의 대부분은 커피나 코코아 같은 기본 작물 같은 것을 생산하는 것으로 알려져 있다. 이러저러한 생산품들은 넓게 거래되고 가난한 나라들에 커다란 이익을 가져온다. 국제노동기구는 2억 4천6백만 어린이들이 전 세계적으로 노동에 투입된다고 말한다. 이들 중에서 8백만은 성을 파도록 강요되고 있다.

최근에 중국의 많은 가난한 아이들이 노예 노동이 강요되어지고 있다고 한다. 8세 정도의 어린 어린이들이 납치되어서 공장이나 벽돌공장에서 일한다. 근로 상태는 종종 위험하고 많은 어린이들이 심각하게 다치거나 죽음을 당한다.

■ Words & Phrases

face: 직면하다
developing countries: 개발도상국가
be forced to: 강제로~ 하게 되다
be fed: 먹여지다
little: 거의~ 없는
toward: ~쪽으로
produce: 만들어내다
trade: 장사하다, 교역하다
profits: 이익, 이득, 수익
ILO: 세계노동기구
million: 백만
be forced into~: 강제로~에 놓여지다
as young as: ~만큼 어린
kidnap: 납치하다, 유괴하다
brickyard: 벽돌공장

■ Grammatical Points

① Child labor is one of the most serious problems faced by developing countries today.

: 'one of+복수명사'는 '~중의 하나'라는 의미이다. faced는 과거분사로 앞에 '관계대명사(which)+be 동사(is)'가 생략되어

있으며 one of the most serious problems를 수식한다.

② The International Labor Organization(ILO) says that over 246 million children are being put to work worldwide.

: 'are being put to work'은 진행 수동태 형태이다. '2억 4천6백만 어린이들이 일을 하는 상황으로 놓여지고 있는 중이다'의 뜻이다.

Speaking Practice

A: You are looking for a summer job. Are you interested in working full time or _____?

여름에 할 일을 찾고 있다는 거죠. 정규직과 아르바이트 중에서 어디에 관심이 있어요?

B: I would like to work _____.

정규직으로 일하고 싶어요.

A: And _____ do you go to school?

어느 학교에 다니고 있죠?

B: The University of Hankuk.

한국 대학교입니다.

A: Oh, yes. I see that on your _____. When will you _____?

오, 그래요. 지원서에 있군요. 언제 졸업하죠?

B: Next February. I only have one semester _____.

내년 2월에요. 한 학기 남았습니다.

A: Do you have any interests or special _____?

흥미나 특별한 기술이 있나요?

B: Well, I can use a computer, and I know how to speak Chinese.

네, 컴퓨터를 사용할 줄 알고, 중국어를 할 줄 알아요.

■ **Words & Phrases**

application: 지원서
semester: 학기
skill: 기술
left: (leave의 과거분사) 남은

■ **Grammatical Points**

Are you interested in working full time or part-time?

: be interested in은 '~에 관심이 있다'의 뜻이다.

I only have one semester left.

: I only have one semester (which is) left의 문장으로서 '주격 관계대명사+be 동사'가 생략되었다. left가 one semester를 수식한다.

Unit

18 Glacier

빙하

Reading Comprehension

Glaciers are the most spectacular of nature features. ① They are like flowing rivers of densely packed ice. Unlike a river, however, a glacier cannot be seen to move. ② But accurate measurements do show that it is flowing. Glacial erosion of bedrock and deposits of the material eroded are characteristic and easily recognizable. ③ Their distribution enables us to infer that in the recent past, ④ glaciers were far more extensive than they are today. At the same time, this evidence has raised questions about the possible causes of the "ice ages."

빙하는 자연 가운데서 가장 장관을 이룬다. 빙하는 조밀하게 뭉쳐진 얼음 덩어리가 강처럼 흘러가는 것과 같다. 그러나 강과는 달리, 빙하가 움직이는 것을 볼 수는 없다. 하지만 정확히 측정해보면 그것이 흐른다는 것을 알 수 있다. 빙하에 의한 기반암의 침식과 침식된 물질의 퇴적물은 특징적이고 쉽게 알아볼 수 있다. 그것들의 분포로 우리는 비교적 최근에도 빙하가 오늘날보다 훨씬 더 광범위했다는 추론을 할 수 있다. 동시에 이러한 증거는 "빙하시대"를 가능케 했던 원인에 대해 궁금증을 불러일으켜 왔다.

■ Words & Phrases

glacier: 빙하
spectacular: 장관인, 구경거리의
feature: (산천 등의) 지형, 특색, 특징
densely: 조밀하게, 빽빽하게
packed: 빽빽하게, 조밀하게
measurement: 측정, 측량
erosion: 침식, 부식 cf. erode (바닷물, 바람 등이)~을 침식하다
bedrock: (지질) 기반암, 근본, 근저
deposit: 퇴적물, 침전물
characteristic: 알아볼 수 있는, 분간할 수 있는
distribution: 분포, 배치
infer: ~을 추론하다, 추리하다
extensive: 넓은 범위에 걸친
ice age: 빙하시대

■ Grammatical Points

① They are like flowing rivers of densely packed ice. Unlike a river, however, a glacier cannot be seen to move.

: like는 '…처럼'의 뜻이다. packed는 과거분사로 ice를 수식한다.

② But accurate measurements do show that it is flowing.

: do는 show를 강조하는 조동사이다.

③ Their distribution enables us to infer~

: enable A to-v는 'A가~하는 것을 가능하게 하다'이다.

④ glaciers were far more extensive than they are today.

: far는 비교급을 수식함으로써 '훨씬'이라는 뜻이다.

Speaking Practice

A: Have you _____ the reports on TV from the countries affected by the tsunami disaster?

해일 재앙이 닥친 나라들에서 찍어 온 TV 리포트 봤니?

B: Yes, I've been really depressed by all the sad stories.

응, 해일 재앙으로 인한 슬픈 소식들 때문에 정말 기운이 없었어.

A: Well, that's _____. Many of the people who live there have lost entire families, and the _____ seemed to be absolutely stunned by the disaster.

이해가 돼. 그들 중 많은 사람들이 자신들의 가족을 모두 잃었어. 그리고 생존자도 재앙으로 인해 몹시 놀랐지.

B: I know. If that had happened to me, I don't know what I would have done.

알아, 그런 일이 나에게 발생한다면 난 어떻게 해야 할지 모를 거야.

A: On the other _____, there have been some incredible survival stories.

반면에 놀라운 생존 이야기들이 있었어.

B: I haven't _____ about those.

난 그건 듣지 못했는데.

A: There was one man who managed to grab and hang on to the top of a tree after the tsunami had carried him inland for more than a kilometer.

해일 때문에 1킬로미터 이상 멀리 쓸려간 후에 간신히 나무를 잡아서 그 나무 꼭대기에 매달려 있던 사람이 있었어.

B: That's _____. He was one of the few lucky ones.

놀랍구나. 그는 운 좋은 몇 사람들 중 하나구나.

■ Words & Phrases

inland: 바다에서 멀리 떨어진
depressed: 의기소침한, 풀이 죽은
understandable: 이해할 수 있는
entire: 전체의, 온전한
incredible: 엄청난, 믿어지지 않는, 대단한
survivor: 살아남은 사람
stun: 기절시키다, 인사불성에 빠뜨리다, 망연하게 하다
on the other hand: 또 한편으로는
disaster: 재난
manage to: 간신히 ~ 하다
grab: 잡아채다
inland: 바다에서 멀리 떨어진

■ Grammatical Points

Have you seen the reports on TV from the countries affected by
the tsunami disaster?

: the countries (which were) affected by the tsunami disaster?
'주격 관계대명사+be 동사'가 생략되었다.

I've been really depressed by all the sad stories.
: 'have been+과거분사'의 형태로 쓰인 현재완료 수동태 문장이다.

※ 현재완료의 수동태

· 현재완료는 'have+과거분사'의 형태로 과거의 일이 현재까지 영향을 미치
  는 경우에 사용된다.
· 현재완료의 수동태는 'have been+과거분사'의 형태로 과거의 일이 현재
  까지 영향을 미치고 있는데, 그 일이 수동적으로 발생했음을 표현할 때 사
  용한다.
  e.g. My car has been stolen.
      (내 차는 도둑맞았다.)
      The toys have been sold quickly.
      (그 장난감들은 빠르게 팔렸다.)
      The play has been loved for 20 years.
      (그 연극은 20년 동안 사랑받아 오고 있다.)

There was one man who managed to grab and hang on to the top
of a tree after the tsunami had carried him inland for more than

a kilometer.

: (대과거) 과거의 어떤 때보다 먼저 일어난 동작은 과거완료로 나타낸다.

쓰나미가 그를 멀리 떠내려 보낸 후(had carried)에 간신히 나무 꼭대기를 잡고 매달렸던 한 남자가 있었다(There was one man who managed to grab and hang~).

He was one of the few lucky ones.

: 'one of 복수명사' 형태이다.

ones는 survivors를 대신한 대명사이다.

19 Greenpeace

그린피스

Reading Comprehension

In 1971, a small boat set sail from Vancouver, Canada. In an act of non-violent protest, ① the ship headed towards Amchitka, one of the Aleutian Islands connecting North American and Asia. Here, the US government was planning to hold a nuclear test. ② The twelve-person crew onboard the Phyllis Cormack aimed to stop the test.

Although the voyage of the Phyllis Cormack did not succeed in its immediate goal, the peaceful demonstration did have one positive result: ③ It attracted worldwide attention and gave birth to the international movement that would be called Greenpeace.

Today, Greenpeace is an international, non-profit organization. It has offices in countries throughout the world.

1971년에 조그만 배가 캐나다 밴쿠버에서 출항했다. 비폭력적인 항의의 행동으로 배가 북미와 아시아를 연결하는 알류산 열도의 한 섬인 Amchitka로 향했다. 이곳에서 미국 정부는 핵실험을 할 계획이었다. Phyllis Cormack에 탑승한 12명의 무리들은 그 실험을 막으려는 작정이었다.

비록 Phyllis Cormack의 항해가 즉각적인 목표를 달성하지는 못했지만 평화로운 시위는 한 긍정적인 결과를 얻었다: 그것은 전 세계적 관심을 끌었고 그린피스라고 불리어지는 국제적인 운동을 탄생시켰다.

오늘날 그린피스는 국제적이고 비영리 조직이다. 그것은 전 세계에 많은 나라에 사무실을 두고 있다.

■ Grammatical Points

① the ship headed towards Amchitka, one of the Aleutian Islands connecting North American and Asia.

: Amchitka와 one of the Aleutian Islands는 동격. (which were) connecting North American and Asia가 Aleutian Islands를 수식한다.

② The twelve-person crew onboard the Phyllis Cormack aimed to stop the test.

: onboard the Phyllis Cormack이 The twelve-person crew(12명의 무리들)을 수식한다.

③ It attracted worldwide attention and gave birth to the international movement that would be called Greenpeace.

: 주격 관계대명사 that이 앞에 있는 명사(선행사)인 the international movement를 수식한다.

Speaking Practice

A: Hi, Isabel. What are you doing?

안녕, 이사벨, 뭐하니?

B: Hi, Jeff. I'm making a poster. Our class is doing a project on global warming for the _____ fair.

안녕, 제프. 지금 포스트 만들고 있어. 우리 반이 과학 박람회를 위한 지구온난화에 대한 프로젝트를 하는 중이야.

A: Great! That's a really _____ problem. Our science class is doing a _____ project right now.

멋지다. 그거 정말 심각한 문제지 우리 과학 수업은 재활용 프로젝트를 하는 중이야.

B: Oh, yeah? What are you doing?

아, 그래? 너희는 뭐하는데?

A: Well, a lot of things. We're talking to our family and friends about recycling and then we're having a contest.

음, 많은 것. 우리는 가족과 친구들에게 재활용에 대해서 이야기해. 그러고 나서 대회를 할 거야.

B: Sounds great. Who can enter?

멋지다. 누가 참가할 수 있니?

A: Anyone can enter. All you need is a group to work with.

아무나 할 수 있어. 그러나 함께할 그룹이 있어야 돼.

B: And what does each group do?

각 그룹들이 무엇을 하는데?

A: They _____ paper and plastic. The groups that collect a lot get a _____.

그들은 종이와 플라스틱을 수집해. 많이 수집한 그룹은 상을 타.

B: Cool. What's the prize?

멋지다, 무슨 상인데?

A: They can go to see the TV show *Save the Planet.*

티비 쇼인 '지구를 구하기'를 보러 갈 수 있어.

■ Words & Phrases

global warming: 지구온난화
fair: 박람회
recycling: 재활용
contest: 대회
enter: 참여하다
collect: 수집하다
prize: 상

■ Grammatical Points

All you need is a group to work with.

: 목적격 관계대명사 that이 생략된 문장으로서 you need가 all을
수식한다. to work with는 to 부정사의 명사적 용법으로서 group
를 수식한다.

the groups that collect a lot get a prize.

: 주어는 the groups으로서 that collect a lot의 수식을 받는다.

Zazz

재즈

Reading Comprehension

Zazz began in the early 1900's as a music of African-Americans. It was intended for singing, for dancing, and for entertainment and atmosphere at parties or social gatherings.

Jazz has continued to develop and has produced some of the

United States' leading singers, instrumentalists, and composers. Today, ① it is considered by many to be America's art music. Jazz represents a blending of musical elements from Africa and from Europe. Jazz uses some European ideas of harmony and melody, but the rhythms are more African in origin.

Another important feature of jazz is improvisation. ② To improvise means to make something up on the spur of the moment. This is the way jazz is usually played. ③ Thus a good jazz soloist seldom plays anything the same way twice.

재즈는 아프리카 미국인들의 음악으로 1900년대 초에 시작되었다. 노래와 춤을 위한, 도는 파티나 사회적 집회의 여흥과 분위기를 위한 것이었다.

재즈는 계속해서 발전하여 미국의 유명 가수들, 연주자들, 작곡가들을 배출하였다. 오늘날 많은 사람들은 재즈가 미국의 예술 음악이 되었다고 생각한다. 재즈는 아프리카와 유럽의 음악적 요소들의 합성을 나타낸다. 재즈는 유럽의 하모니와 멜로디 개념을 일부 사용하지만, 리듬의 기원은 더욱 아프리카적이다.

재즈의 또 다른 중요한 특징은 즉흥연주이다. 즉흥적으로 한다는 것은 어떤 것을 즉석에서 해내는 것을 의미한다. 그래서 훌륭한 재즈 독주자는 어떤 것도 같은 방식으로 두 번 다시 연주하는 일이 좀체 없다.

intend: 의도하다
atmosphere: 분위기
social gathering: 사회적 집회
continue: 계속하다, 연속하다
develop: 발전하다
leading: 주요한
instrumentalist: 연주자
be considered: ~로 여겨지다
composer: 작곡가
represent: 표현하다, 나타내다, 묘사하다
blending: 혼합, 융합
element: 요소
in origin: 태생
feature: 특질
improvisation: 즉흥 연구, 즉석 연기 improvise v. 즉흥으로 연주하다
make up: 꾸미다
spur of the moment: 충동적으로 앞뒤 가리지 않고, 돌연히, 당장에
seldom: 좀처럼~ 않다

■ Grammatical Points

① it is considered by many to be America's art music.

: Many consider that it is America's art music의 수동태 형식이다.

② To improvise means to make something up on the spur of the moment.

: To improvise는 주어로 쓰인 to 부정사의 명사적 용법이고 to make something up은 보어로 쓰인 to 부정사의 명사적 용법이다.

This is the way jazz is usually played.

: 선행사가 the way라서 현대 영어에서 관계부사 how를 함께 쓰지 않는다. the way 혹은 how만을 쓰든지, the way that 혹은 the way in which를 쓴다.

  e.g. Tell me the way you solved the problem.

    Tell me how you solved the problem.

    Tell me the way that you solved the problem.

    Tell me the way in which you solved the problem.

    (네가 그 문제를 푼 방법을 내게 말해 다오.)

③ **Thus a good jazz soloist seldom plays anything the same way twice.**

  : 빈도부사 seldom은 be 동사 뒤 일반 동사 앞에 온다.

Speaking Practice

A: Oh, the concert was quite good, wasn't it?

오, 콘서트 정말 좋았지, 그렇지?

B: Well… the concert itself was generally good, but something was
_____ me.

어, 콘서트 자체는 대체로 좋았는데, 그러나 신경 쓰이는 것이
있었어.

A: What was that?

무엇이었는데?

B: Ringing phones. I don't understand why people don't turn ___
their cell phone during a concert!

전화가 울린 것. 나는 왜 사람들이 콘서트 중에 셀폰을 끄지 않

는지 이해가 안 돼.

A: Actually, I was bothered by that, too. Some people don't care about others.

사실, 나는 그것 때문에 짜증났어. 어떤 사람들은 남들을 상관하지 않아.

B: You're right. I think people should put their phones on _____ mode or turn them off in public _____ like a concert hall or a movie theater.

네 말이 맞아. 사람들은 전화들을 무음으로 놓거나 콘서트홀이나 영화관 같은 공공장소에서는 꺼야 한다고 생각해.

A: I totally agree _____ you.

전적으로 공감해.

■ Words & Phrases

generally: 일반적으로, 보편적으로
bother: 괴롭히다, 귀찮게 하다
ring: (소리가) 울리다, 울려 퍼지다
turn off: (가스, 라디오, tv, 수돗물) 끄다
like: ~와 같은
care: 신경 쓰다
silent mode: 묵음모드
totally: 전적으로

■ Grammatical Points

the concert was quite good, wasn't it?

: (부가의문문) 평서문 뒤에 짧게 덧붙인 의문문으로, 이것은 특히 구어에 쓰인다. 일반적으로 긍정문 뒤에는 부정의문문을, 부정문 뒤에는 긍정의문문을 덧붙인다.

e.g. <u>Tom is diligent</u>, <u>isn't he</u>? [Tom → he]
　　　긍정문　　　　부정문

　　<u>Your sister isn't tall</u>, <u>is she</u>? [Your sister → she]
　　　　부정문　　　　긍정문

　　You go to church, don't you? (너는 교회에 다니지?)

　　You don't go to church, do you? (너는 교회에 다니지 않지?)

Answers

Unit 1.
Speaking Practice

A: Do you know what the most important <u>quality</u> of a successful person is?

B: I'm not <u>sure</u>, but I think <u>honesty</u> is the key to success.

A: You know what everybody says nowadays?

B: I don't know. What?

A: Creativity is the <u>key</u> to success.

B: I guess you're right. I'm afraid I'm not a very <u>creative</u> person.

A: You just have to find your <u>hidden</u> talents.

B: What do you think my hidden <u>talents</u> are?

A: I think you're <u>good</u> at writing and making stories.

Unit 2.
Speaking Practice

A: Do you know what an <u>aged</u> society is?

B: If the <u>ratio</u> of seniors aged 65 or older <u>against</u> the total population is over 14%, it is considered an aged society.

A: What <u>about</u> Korea? Are we an aged society or an <u>aging</u> society?

B: Korea became an aging society in 2000. But we are <u>approaching</u> the status of "aged society" very rapidly.

A: Wow. You seem very <u>knowledgeable</u> about that.

B: In fact, I just read about in the newspaper. Experts <u>predict</u> Korea will become an aged society in 19 years.

A: Are other countries aging as <u>quickly</u> as ours?

B: No, it says that it <u>took</u> 24 years for Japan <u>to</u> change from an aging to an aged society and 115 years for France. So I guess we are a rapidly aging group.

Unit 3.
Speaking Practice

A: Excuse me, My phone stopped <u>working</u> yesterday all of a sudden and I am not sure <u>why</u>. Do you think you could take a <u>look</u> at it?

B: Have you tried <u>resetting</u> it?

A: Resetting it? Oh no, I haven't actually. How do you reset Nokia phones anyway?

B: You just have to <u>press</u> these two side buttons at the <u>same</u> time and there you have it. It should come on now. Aha. there you go—everything should be working again now.

A: That's <u>it</u>? Wow, you really have the magic touch. Thank you so much.

Unit 4.
Speaking Practice

A: What do you usually <u>do</u> on weekends?

B: Nothing <u>special</u>. I stay home all <u>day</u>.

A: Don't you go <u>out</u>?

B: Rarely. I'm usually <u>too</u> tired <u>to</u> go out. Besides, Sunday is my only day <u>off</u>, so I have to clean the house, do the <u>laundry</u> and other <u>chores</u>.

A: The Koreans work too hard. I feel <u>sorry</u> for you.

B: But I <u>prefer</u> to stay home and do little things around the house. I especially enjoy <u>working</u> in my garden. I <u>grow</u> many kinds of flowers.

Unit 5.
Speaking Practice

A: What's for <u>lunch</u> today?

B: Well··· I have no <u>idea</u>. What would you <u>like</u>?

A: Well. I really feel like seafood spaghetti.

B: But we are missing one important <u>ingredient</u>. There's no seafood <u>left</u> in the fridge.

A: Don't worry. I'll go buy some seafood right now if you decide to make it.

B: Okay! I'll do it, but it will <u>take</u> at least 30 minutes to <u>cook</u>.

A: No problem. I'll go to a <u>seafood</u> store right away. Where are the car keys?

B: On the television in the living room. Ah, go to the store next to the post office. They <u>sell</u> really fresh seafood.

A: Okay, I will.

Unit 6.
Speaking Practice

Susie: Jane, I can't thank you <u>enough</u> for the bridal <u>shower</u> you had for me!

Mary: What does bridal shower mean?

Susie: Bridal showers are given by <u>close</u> friends of the bride to be as a sort of dowry. The shower gifts are usually the domestic variety, such as linens and kitchen utensils.

Jane: My <u>pleasure</u>! You really got some lovely gifts. Those kitchen utensils will sure come in handy.

Susie: Well. I guess I'll now have to learn how to <u>cook</u>.

Unit 7.
Speaking Practice

Doctor: Well, Mrs. Pak, I've <u>completed</u> my examination and I'm happy to say it's nothing <u>serious.</u>

Mrs. Pak: Don't you think you should <u>take</u> X-rays?

Doctor: I don't think X-rays will be <u>necessary</u> for this illness.

Mrs. Pak: It's a <u>contagious</u> disease, isn't it?

Doctor: You have the <u>flu</u>.

Mrs. Pak: Can I be <u>cured</u> easily?

Doctor: Yes, You listen to my advice and I'm certain you'll be fine.

Mrs. Pak: What <u>should</u> I do?

Doctor: <u>Take</u> this medicine <u>every</u> four hours and get <u>plenty</u> of rest. There's nothing to worry <u>about</u>.

Unit 8.
Speaking Practice

A: How <u>about</u> some coffee?

B: That's a great idea. I feel dead <u>tired</u>.

A: Where <u>shall</u> we go?

B: Oh, we don't have to go anywhere. There is a coffee <u>machine</u> around that corner.

A: Okay, Here is a thousand won.

B: Oh, no! This machine is out of <u>order</u>. And I can't get my money back.

A: <u>Forget</u> it. Let's go to the coffee shop <u>across</u> the street.

Unit 9.
Speaking Practice

A: What kind of shoes would you <u>like</u>, ma'am? We have various <u>kinds</u> of shoes. Would you like some dress shoes or just casual <u>ones</u>?

B: Well, I'm looking <u>for</u> some walking shes. Would suede shoes be good for that?

A: Yes, they would, but perhaps calfskin shoes would be the <u>best</u>.

B: Okay. Could you show me several <u>pairs</u> of each kind?

A: Certainly, ma'am. What' your <u>size</u>, please?

B: Seven and a half.

A: Here's a pair in your size. They are very good for the price.

B: Could I <u>try</u> them on?

A: Certainly⋯. How do they <u>feel</u>?

B: Well, they're a little <u>tight.</u>

Unit 10.
Speaking Practice

A: How do I look <u>in</u> this jacket?

B: You <u>look</u> very good. I think this blue jacket <u>suits</u> you better than the black <u>one</u>.

A: I think so, too. So how much is this jacket?

B: Its <u>regular</u> price is $200, but it's 10% <u>off</u> right now.

A: That sounds good. Okay, I'll buy this jacket.

B: How would you like to <u>pay</u>?

A: My credit card. Here is the···. Oh, where's my <u>wallet</u>?

B: Is something wrong?

A: I'm sorry, but I think I <u>left</u> my wallet in the car. I have to go back to the parking <u>lot</u>.

B: No problem. It often happens to <u>customers</u>.

Unit 11.
Speaking Practice

A: You look <u>pale</u>. What <u>happened</u>?

B: I didn't sleep <u>a wink</u> last night.

A: Did you have something on your mind? You look so <u>concerned</u>!

B: Well, I'm <u>under</u> a lot of pressure. My boss is very <u>pushy</u>. He <u>assigned</u> me three projects. Now the <u>deadlines</u> are near and I still haven't finished all of my projects.

A: Is there <u>anything</u> I can do to help you?

B: Well, I guess no one can help me <u>but</u> myself. For the moment, I just need someone to talk to so that I can <u>relieve</u> my stress.

Unit 12.
Speaking Practice

A: I have no <u>energy</u> and I'm tired all the time. What's <u>wrong</u> with me, doctor?

B: Are you eating nutritious meals three <u>times</u> a day?

A: Well, not really. I'm so busy that I often only have a quick <u>snack</u> between classes.

B: I see. And what about <u>physical</u> activity?

A: As I said, I'm busy. I've got no time.

B: You will simply have to take time <u>off</u> from your schedule to eat good meals and to exercise. <u>Otherwise</u>, you'll end up in serious trouble.

Unit 13.
Speaking Practice

A: Were you <u>surprised</u> that I dressed up? It's Halloween. (October 31)

B: Halloween?

A: Yes, we usually dress up as ghosts and monsters and go round to people's houses asking, "Trick or Treat." Can you figure out what I mean?

B: Yes, a little. What if the children do not get a treat?

A: They usually soap the windows. It's a trick.

B: That's funny! Do they have any parties, too?

A: Of course. During the party they usually play games such as getting apples out of water using only their mouth.

Unit 14.
Speaking Practice

A: You look so tired. What happened?

B: I only slept for four hours last night.

A: Oh, that's too bad. Getting enough sleep is very important.

B: If I don't get eight hours sleep, I'm tired the whole next day.

A: What kept you awake for so long? Exams?

B: You got it. I'm so stressed out about exams that I usually sleep for five hours these days. What should I do?

A: You should learn how to relax.

Unit 15.
Speaking Practice

A: What's <u>for</u> dinner?

B: Let's get hamburgers.

A: We just <u>had</u> one yesterday. We can't eat hamburgers every day.

B: But I don't want to <u>cook</u> today.

A: Look, eating <u>junk</u> food is not good for our health if we eat it often.

B: You mean that we're going to get sick if we don't stop <u>eating</u> hamburgers? Can you really quit <u>eating</u> fast food for <u>good</u>? No more tomato sauce, cheese, and French fries for the rest of your life?

A: I don't think I said that, exactly. But since we've just eaten junk food, for the time being we shouldn't have any more. That's what I <u>mean</u>.

B: Okay. then I'll cook today.

Unit 16.
Speaking Practice

A: I heard that you're <u>interested</u> in environmentally friendly products.

B: Yes, I've been using those products to <u>conserve</u> the environment. Why do you ask?

A: I saw a really interesting documentary on new developments in technology last night.

B: I'm sorry I <u>missed</u> that.

A: The one that really made me surprised was a prototype battery made from spinach.

B: Spinach! That's a vegetable. I don't believe it.

A: It's true. They can engineer spinach cells to <u>convert</u> light into electricity to power something like a laptop computer.

B: That's <u>incredible</u>.

Unit 17.
Speaking Practice

A: You are looking for a summer job. Are you interested in working full time or <u>part-time</u>?

B: I would like to work <u>full-time</u>.

A: And <u>where</u> do you go to school?

B: The University of Hankuk.

A: Oh, yes. I see that on your <u>application</u>. When will you <u>graduate</u>?

B: Next February. I only have one semester <u>left.</u>

A: Do you have any interests or special <u>skills</u>?

B: Well, I can use a computer, and I know how to speak Chinese.

Unit 18.
Speaking Practice

A: Have you <u>seen</u> the reports on TV from the countries affected by the tsunami disaster?

B: Yes, I've been really depressed by all the sad stories.

A: Well, that's <u>understandable</u>. Many of the people who live there have lost entire families, and the <u>survivors</u> seemed to be absolutely stunned by the disaster.

B: I know. If that had happened to me, I don't know what I would have done.

A: On the other hand, there have been some incredible survival stories.

B: I haven't <u>heard</u> about those.

A: There was one man who managed to grab and hang on to the top of a tree after the tsunami had carried him inland for more than a kilometer.

B: That's <u>amazing</u>. He was one of the few lucky ones.

Unit 19.
Speaking Practice

A: Hi, Isabel. What are you doing?

B: Hi, Jeff. I'm making a poster. Our class is doing a project on global warming for the science fair.

A: Great! That's a really _serious_ problem. Our science class is doing a _recycling_ project right now.

B: Oh, yeah? What are you doing?

A: Well, a lot of things. We're talking to our family and friends about recycling and then we're having a contest.

B: Sounds great. Who can enter?

A: Anyone can enter. All you need is a group to work with.

B: And what does each group do?

A: They _collect_ paper and plastic. The groups that collect a lot get a prize.

B: Cool. What's the prize?

A: They can go to see the TV show _Save the Planet._

Unit 20.
Speaking Practice

A: Oh, the concert was quite good, wasn't it?

B: Well··· the concert itself was generally good, but something was _bothering_ me.

A: What was that?

B: Ringing phones. I don't understand why people don't turn _off_ their cell phone during a concert!

A: Actually, I was bothered by that, too. Some people don't care about others.

B: You're right. I think people should put their phones on <u>silent</u> mode or turn them off in public <u>places</u> like a concert hall or a movie theater.

A: I totally <u>agree</u> with you.

정효숙

성신여자대학교 영어영문학과 졸업
성신여자대학교 대학원 영문학 석사
경희대학교 경영대학원 관광경영학 석사
숭실대학교 영문학 박사(드라마 전공)
현) 한영신학대학교 선교영어학과 교수

『호텔영어』
『릴리언 헬먼의 작품에 나타난 젠더 역할 연구』
『쉽게 배우는 영작문』
『열린 영어회화』(1, 2)
『(회화가 술술 되는) 기초 영작문』
「Shakespeare의 Plutarch 연구」
「Between Comedy and Tragedy: Measure for Measure, All's Well that Ends Well을 중심으로」
「Death of a Salesman과 The Crucible에 나타난 여성인물 연구」
「성역할의 관점에서 본 Albee의 Martha에 관한 연구」 외 다수

College 2
English

초판인쇄 2017년 6월 30일
초판발행 2017년 6월 30일

지은이 정효숙
펴낸이 채종준
펴낸곳 한국학술정보㈜
주소 경기도 파주시 회동길 230(문발동)
전화 031) 908-3181(대표)
팩스 031) 908-3189
홈페이지 http://ebook.kstudy.com
전자우편 출판사업부 publish@kstudy.com
등록 제일산-115호(2000. 6. 19)

ISBN 978-89-268-7688-6 93740